STUDIES IN FRENCH LITERATURE No. 13

Emeritus Fellow

DATE DUE FOR RETURN

General Editor

W. C. Moore

of St John's College, Oxford

BEAUMARCHAIS:
LE BARBIER DE SÉVILLE

by
ROBERT NIKLAUS

Professor of French and Italian
University of Exeter

EDWARD ARNOLD

© ROBERT NIKLAUS 1968

First published 1968 by
Edward Arnold (Publishers) Ltd.,
25 Hill Street, London W1X 8LL
Reprinted 1972, 1975

ISBN: 0 7131 5519 1

Printed in Great Britain by
The Camelot Press Ltd, Southampton

Contents

I

One hundred and ninety years after its first performance, the curtain is still rising upon the *Barbier de Séville* (1775); and throughout this long period audiences have discovered different criteria of enjoyment, according to the inevitable changes in modes of thought and behaviour.

Part of its appeal today may well be due to its revelation, in authentic terms, of the *Ancien Régime*, the superbly theatrical period that reached its apogée in the seventeenth century, and disappeared in a welter of agony and destruction in 1789, some fourteen years after *Le Barbier de Séville* first appeared. The play contains explosively the quintessence of the tragedy to come: the brilliant sophistication, the exquisite refinement of manner and mode, the elegant good taste that for so many years cast a deceptive glow over the cruelty, indifference and ruthless egoism of the masters.

Another part of this lasting appeal reaches over the years, its immediate impact only slightly attenuated today. Beaumarchais set his play in Seville; and his first audience deeply enjoyed their vicarious entry into a country whose exotic flavour had been made familiar to them through picaresque accounts of life and love in the torrid climate of Spain as well as through abounding translations from the Spanish. Spain was at that time fashionable, exciting, rediscovered, filled with all the glamour of unknown places.

Le Barbier de Séville is lit with the burning sun and cold clear moon of a Spain that is not quite real, yet readily accepted by all those who enter in, then as now. It is an imaginary land of fierce romantic love affairs, conducted according to the rules in a businesslike and calculating manner, in strange contrast to their apparent full-blooded and heedless passion. 'Affaires de cœur' is now a commonplace term, but when Regnard first coined it, it was an exact and witty description of these intrigues. So Beaumarchais sets his scene to the scent of roses, the nostalgic sound of guitars beating plaintively against the jealously guarded closed shutters above shadowed balconies, fully aware of the power of the evocative atmosphere of love behind bars waiting to break free, so familiar and so strange to those who watched and waited.

There is a duality about the scene that is in itself promise of the pleasure to come. All the elements of this unreal and totally acceptable Spain are present. Yet Dr Bartholo's house in this sunlit street in Seville is distinctively eighteenth-century French, in spite of the Spanish grille over the shuttered windows. It symbolises the knowledge shared by the first audiences, and all those who have subsequently watched the play. In spite of all the Spanish airs and graces that adorn the *Barbier*, the real terms of reference are French; the intellectual, psychological and emotional climate is that of eighteenth-century France. The Spanish trappings free the imagination to accept any fantasy or improbability within the highly involved action of an exceptionally swift moving play.

The simple and effective setting of a street of closed and shuttered houses, however common to the age, enabled Beaumarchais to make full use of the stage. The action of the play moves freely and rapidly from one point to another without breaking the unity of place, without any slackening of pace or impeding of the easy flowing of the plot. An impression is given of diversity of movement and character, of intensive activity building to a climax unknown as yet, and unbroken even by the swift scene change at the beginning of Act II, from the street to Rosine's chamber. A noticeable factor in building the atmosphere of the play is the barred and curtained windows which, whether seen from the outside in the street, or from within the room, create a sultry feeling of foreboding, of latent drama and suspense.

It is a simple setting that evokes a complex response; and this is, in effect, the keynote of a complex play deployed with every appearance of artless simplicity.

Consider the first appearance of the Count Almaviva.

The curtain rises upon an apparently empty street; but there, lurking in the shadow, is a furtive and sinister figure, muffled in a dark cloak, his face concealed beneath the turned-down brim of his hat. Restlessly pacing up and down, looking at his watch, talking aloud in the empty street, he is a disturbed and disturbing enigma, exciting and mysterious; and his swift pacing to and fro immediately establishes the tempo of the play, breathtaking throughout with its exceptional speed and fluency, that never falters or sags.

The enigma is presented to us through the oldest of all traditional devices. In the course of the play, Beaumarchais made use of every known theatrical device, and none more brilliantly than in the opening scene when the Count appears in disguise. As the primitive hunter assumed the likeness of his prey to gain power over it through sympathetic magic, so Almaviva assumes a different persona to gain amorous power over Rosine.

The essence of the comedy here lies in the nature of the disguise, and the way in which the enigma is resolved: for the sinister cloak and wide-brimmed hat, the traditional costume of the conspirator in the theatre, are seen to be the robes and hat of an Abbé. So the Count is, with his first appearance, robbed of his splendour, and the memory of this lingers even when the disguise is discarded. The satin and laces and jewels of the privileged aristocrat are covered by dingy clerical robes. These demand the reverse of his normal air of arrogant assurance, the graceful stride of the man who walks on his own land, secure in the power of his birth and wealth. It is, therefore, an added delight as the scene progresses to watch him stumbling and shuffling around, his proud shoulders humbly bowed, depressed into what he believes to be the likeness of a priest.

There is, beyond the obvious disguise, another more subtle and more comic, and one arising from the demands of the sophisticated audiences of eighteenth-century France. For Beaumarchais kept one eye trained upon his public; and every *trompe-l'œil* effect he creates is dedicated to their satisfaction. Nothing could please them better than the feeling of *dépaysement*, to which Marivaux had accustomed an earlier generation of playgoers with his delightful vistas of a fairy's garden, an enchanted meadow, a distant island shimmering in the sun—aspects of a never-never land of his own invention. In a similar way, the Count's reference to 'un Espagnol du temps d'Isabelle', an improvement upon Beaumarchais' first 'du temps de Charles Quint', opens up appreciable vistas. It is clear that he is all set to play the part of a Spaniard of that much earlier period.

Under the great Queen Isabella (1451-1504) it was right and proper to appear ingenuous and naïve, to sigh for the love of a lady one had never met: much in the same way that Elizabethan poets addressed their love lyrics to the Virgin Queen. In that golden age of Isabella, expressions of sensual feeling were simple and direct. The Count adopts this earlier romanticism because he believes that it will be more appealing to an inexperienced young girl and so make her seduction easier of accomplishment. It is certain that this return to a romanticism so remote from the brilliant cynicism and sophistication of eighteenth-century France would bring about an enjoyable suspension of reality for the audience, and constitute in itself a fertile source of comedy.

Moreover, since the Count is very much the aristocrat of his age, in no way resembling the blunt and straightforward Spaniard at the Court of Isabella, he needs a very good disguise indeed to cover his own more complex and more decadent intentions. And he is given the best. There is nothing in him at all of the religious man; and for the audience there was the added delight, with more than a touch of malice in it, of watching the supposedly passionate and romantic young lover in the guise of a doddering old Abbé. Beaumarchais' anti-clericalism declared itself at the outset by this choice, and he clearly relied upon a similar attitude of mind in his audience to illumine the full humour of the situation; for this very dubious Abbé is seen skulking in the shadows for purposes of amorous intrigue: the contrast between the chastity of his attire and the profligacy of his intentions is irresistibly comic.

Brief and brilliant use is made of the conventional soliloquy. In a few lines, ill-assorted with his appearance, the Count expresses his intentions concerning Rosine, and in so doing introduces the play, sets it in place and time, and reveals himself, even when he has most need to hide himself, in all his arrogance, egoism, sensuality, decadence and world-weary lassitude. The décor, the disguise, the soliloquy take his audience into a world of unreality, of fantasy and artifice very much to their taste; so is the sophistry of his speech, lightly masquerading as philoso-phy, and common to Beaumarchais and to most of his fellow French-men. 'Chacun court après son bonheur' is not only an axiom, but also a truism, and here serves to justify the Count in his immoral pursuits. He shows himself experienced, proud of his easy conquests even while he deplores the satiety they bring; and determined to win Rosine. 'Il est si doux d'être aimé pour soi-même' he sighs, heavily disguised as someone he is not, and determined to win her by every duplicity in the book.

The approach of Figaro sends the Count scuttling back into the sha-dows like some grotesque cockroach disturbed by the light. For Figaro the barber is an effulgent sun. There is no shadow nor darkness about him. Though no detail of his costume is given in the manuscript of the play, the earliest printed editions show the dress which has since and quite properly become traditional: for it is the physical presentation of the spirit of the man, his abundant vitality, his wit, his gaiety, his extrovert and ardent personality as frank and true as the Count's is secret and false.

Figaro is an arresting figure the moment he comes on stage. He is a Spaniard: his netted hair clubbed at the back and his large white hat, the cut of his jacket and his breeches, his flowing silk kerchief make this manifest. Yet he is like no Spaniard who ever existed. The gay colours of his jacket, lined to match his flamboyant waistcoat, have a jaunty glitter that is all Figaro. Even his white stockings and grey shoes are lit up by splendid garters. Like all successfully dramatic costumes, Figaro's carries with it the hint of others—Molière's *Scapin* and the *Arlequin* of Italian Comedy—and these ghostly reminders remain in the minds of the spectators. There is nothing of the humble barber, the artisan, about him; but a great deal of the *petit maître* in his brilliant plumage and his assurance.

The juxtaposition of the Count, his splendour dimmed by the clerical robes he has assumed, hiding in the silent shadows; and of the low-born Figaro in his vivid and jaunty dress dominating the stage as he strums on his guitar and sings with a joyous heart the epicurean ditty he only could have composed, is a dramatic presentation of the changed nature of the dying Master-Servant relationship. For here Figaro is master and immediately sympathetic; while the audience has already laughed at, but not with, the Master.

While the Count was introduced wholly concerned with his own desires, Figaro is presented in the throes of creative travail in a scene of fine comedy. Composer and librettist, he is trying to find words to accompany his tune, instead of setting words to music, counting on the melody to muffle any verbal inadequacy. So his sudden bursts of full-throated song are constantly pulled down by his desperate search for words. Beaumarchais again makes use of the convention of soliloquy, and for the same purpose of revelation of personality and basic motivation. Yet now it is richer, because Figaro's extraordinary exuberance is richer. He is so filled with youth and the joy of living that it bursts from him in all directions like a firecracker newly lit. As Beaumarchais, he is more concerned with life than with art, so that his creative struggles somewhat resemble the convulsions of a mountain giving birth to a mouse. He is not striving after perfection, but after the quick and easy effect. He speaks with his creator's voice when he says—'Aujourd'hui ce qui ne vaut pas la peine d'être dit, on le chante.'

On one level his song is of no significance, a ridiculous jingle without literary or other merit:—

> *Bannissons le chagrin,*
> *Il nous consume :*
> *Sans le feu du bon vin*
> *Qui nous rallume ;*
> *Réduit à languir,*
> *L'homme sans plaisir*
> *Vivrait comme un sot,*
> *Et mourrait bientôt.*

But nothing in this play is on one level only, and nothing is insignificant. Properly understood, Figaro's composition is a total revelation. The first verse reveals his hedonistic philosophy of life. The composition of the lines following demonstrates his easy satisfaction with his own work. His delightfully witty commentary on alternative renderings show him to be experienced in, but not brought down by, the vagaries of human kind. And the inspiration that attends the final spurting of his limited literary genius brings with its verbal juxtaposition of 'cœur'—'maîtresse'—'serviteur', a prescience of the core of the play:—

> *Le vin et la paresse*
> *Se partagent mon cœur ;*
> *Si l'une est ma maîtresse,*
> *L'autre est mon serviteur.*

The last line, three times repeated, is simple only on the surface. In them Figaro recognizes his self-indulgent nature, but asserts his mastery over it; falsely accuses himself of laziness, and so implies that he can make good use of deceptive appearances. For in fact, Figaro, like Beaumarchais, lives a life of unremitting activity, and finds real pleasure in so doing. It is his superabundant energy that gives the play its fantastic tempo: everything he does, he does quickly and with all his heart and mind and spirit. The thrice repeated reference to his laziness and his mastery of it would seem then to imply that he can turn even his defects to advantage, or maybe simulate those he does not in fact possess in order to secure his own fortunes and pleasure. Yet it goes beyond these premisses into the realm of paradox. Figaro's philosophy of life revealed throughout the play, is totally hedonistic, and his ideal way of life would be to do absolutely nothing. So urgent is this desire that even his inborn laziness must be subordinated to it: and so, to achieve his *dolce far niente*, he is prepared to engage in all necessary activities to bring it about, in a ceaseless battle to acquire status and fortune enough for a paradise of endless slothful days. This double revelation, one close upon the heels of the other, by the Count and by Figaro of their intention to pursue happiness at all costs, the statement of the one amplified in the song of the other, sets the tone of the play and presents the special ambivalence that is perhaps its most original element. For Figaro makes it clear that servants as well as masters have a way of life, and seek to attain strangely similar ends. There is nothing of the serf in his attitude or his mind.

As the scene progresses, Figaro reveals himself in all his many parts, and establishes his natural superiority over his master so effortlessly that his first audiences must have accepted the idea of it before they realised its import and audacity. The contributory factors to this ease are essentially dramatic. The two stand on stage together, the one ill at ease in his voluminous disguise, more than a little ridiculous, unwilling to explain his presence there; the other comfortable in his flamboyant dress, perfectly at ease, willing to explain anything to anybody at anytime. The Count is made small and furtive: Figaro larger than life, dominating the stage with his pulsating *élan vital*. Their dialogue, too, points to the same conclusion; for the Count is bound by the stereotype of his class, by his uneasiness and by his purpose. Figaro is bound by nothing. From his first witty comment, with all its satiric overtones, 'Eh non, ce n'est pas un abbé. Cet air altier et noble . . .', he takes the pace of the scene into his own hands. The verve and sparkle of his speech, its swift rhythmic patterns, soaring climaxes and laughter-making throw-away lines, his wry experienced commentary, outclass the Count at every point.

Throughout, Figaro, with nothing to hide, gives himself away with joyous abandon, and from the brilliant fireworks a character in depth emerges: an intelligent man, a man without illusions concerning his fellow men or the society in which he lives, experienced but not cast down, accepting what comes with every intention of turning it to his own ends. To some degree a fatalist, he nevertheless intends to shape his own destiny in spite of initial disadvantages of birth and lack of fortune; and he never doubts the outcome. The assurance of the Count is based upon extraneous factors—birth, breeding, wealth and social prestige. Figaro's assurance is based upon self-confidence, and so is unshakeable. Like all hedonists he is egocentric, and vain. Yet even his dubious characteristics are made acceptable, because of his warm humanity and, above all, his enormous lust for life, his dynamic essence. His strength lies in the fact that he is neither servant nor master: he is a man of liberty, so that he can become the willing accomplice of a former master without becoming his servant, even as to further his own ends he became a barber, without any loss of personal dignity.

In the nineteenth-century, most critics decided that Figaro represented the mouthpiece of the *Tiers Etat*, and that his purpose within the play was to project a man striving to free the masses from an intolerable political yoke, expressing throughout their manifold grievances. But to see him as a figure of political propaganda is to miss his real stature. The power and the danger of Figaro within the society of his time is that he is a manifestly free man. His peculiar creative force, symbolized by his apparently simple but very subtle little song, puts him into a class of his own. In the past he was a servant: it has left no mark upon him. He will become a servant again, but always upon his own terms and for his own ends. In a world of underlings, he towers above them like a Colossus; even more important, he is still a Colossus in the world of masters. His true meaning stems from this natural superiority as a human being. He is no evangelist, no crusader for any causes but his own. Beaumarchais bestowed upon him the gift of a free soul; and the rest followed, for, being free, he spoke aloud with spontaneous wit and dazzling fluency the thoughts that no one else had dared give voice to concerning the injustices and anomalies of his day: not to overthrow the *Ancien Régime*, but because his nature, his intelligence, and his experience made him aware of its monstrous tyranny.

II

'Il est si doux d'être aimé pour soi-même' sighs the Count in the opening scene; and the tone of the play, with its equivocal morality, is set with this speech. The obstinate and insatiable search for personal happiness, the result of complex and essentially selfish motivation, is made apparent from the beginning, and the pseudo-Spanish setting in which the play takes place increasingly assumes new significance. By seeming to satirize foreign ways Beaumarchais is able to call French prejudices to account, a duality that would delight his audiences as it revealed the relativity of moral values, and the fact that all men are brothers under the skin. The choice of Seville for the setting of this comedy has the same effect as the Greek setting for Racine's tragedies, or the modern presentation of hell in Sartre's *Huis Clos*. By a subtle process of alienation, brought about by superimposing a profoundly French content upon an acquired foreignness, dramatic values are enhanced, and the distance achieved ensures that everything is looked upon with new eyes.

So Beaumarchais, writing ostensibly about a passionate Spanish grandee, could deal mortal blows to his French counterpart by holding Almaviva up to ridicule before élite audiences who in themselves represented the society he was deriding. He was able to reveal all facets of a dubious morality without seeming to call his own society to account. Beaumarchais expressed his moral judgement simply by making the Count and Figaro share the same hedonist philosophy, the same determination to achieve their own pleasure by no matter what means and without any regard for the rights of others. By setting them down in a street in Seville, he left open every escape route for himself and others. He did more. He surrounded them with all the colourful trappings of fantasy and unreality in an apparently real world. By suspending belief, he drew his eager audiences into the glittering make-believe world they loved, where their sceptical and sophisticated minds could roam at will. In this foreign land, and in the person of Figaro the barber of Seville, with his spontaneity and his gaiety of heart, his rapid fire of staccato wise cracks and his brilliant commentary on life as he saw it, he offered them the truth about France and Frenchmen everywhere; and this included themselves and their own way of life.

The use of the Spanish Convention in eighteenth-century French literature has a long and imperfectly recorded history, and stems perhaps from the discovery of Cervantes, and the several later parodies of his picaresque epic. *Gil Blas* of Lesage is a perfect example of this kind. Gil Blas, as Figaro does, wanders through life determined to survive in the jungle, turning his hand to any vocation or trade, including that of barber, which comes his way. He too is ready to take advantage of any chance that offers, and is equally determined to enjoy the fruits of this earth to the full. Gil Blas, like Figaro, is presented as a Spaniard, yet remains incontrovertibly French. It is possible that Lesage provided in his novel a background on which both dramatist and spectator might draw to enrich the overtones of the play. Both he and Beaumarchais, in their different ways, offer a sort of *Pilgrims' Progress* of the eighteenth century.

There is, throughout the eighteenth century in France, a tendency among certain of its writers to set their satirical commentaries, in whatsoever form they took, in foreign lands, with Spain as favourite at first, owing to political connexions, and even more perhaps to the exotic qualities bestowed upon it by those nurtured on its literature. But Montesquieu's *Lettres Persanes* enjoyed enormous success, and his bogus Persians served their author well. Voltaire in his *Lettres Philosophiques* directed his satiric barbs against his fellow countrymen while seeming to write about England, and so stimulated an interest in using foreign lands to dissimulate local colour and criticism of the home front. Both Montesquieu and Voltaire pointed their satire by perfecting a light, witty style; and this in turn became part of Beaumarchais' heritage, though he used it differently: for in his play there is no specific satiric intent. He, like his creation Figaro, is carried along by his own wit, and satire results from it, part of a complex compounded of conventions, characters, ideas, situations and ethics, where nothing is what it seems, and everything is deliberately off balance.

We need never doubt the deliberation. Critics have claimed authenticity for the Spain and the Spaniards of Beaumarchais. They have pointed out that in the year 1764-65 he did in fact visit Madrid. The ostensible reason for his visit was to save, somewhat belatedly, the honour of his dearly loved sister Marie Louise whom he liked to call Lisette. She had been abandoned by her lover, Don José Clavijo y Faxardo, and Beaumarchais the devoted brother went to bring her home. He took time off to further his own economic and political schemes while he was there; and also to conduct a successful affair with 'an exalted lady of quality' whom he intended to make, presumably at some future and more convenient date, the mistress of the King. No doubt these several concerns, and his anxiety over his sister, prevented thorough exploration of the town. It is certain that there is no trace at all of the real Spain in this play. Figaro and Almaviva are Spanish by name but French by nature. To insist, against the evidence, on the authenticity of the setting, is to misunderstand Beaumarchais' purpose in using it, which is to lull his spectators with unreality and, paradoxically, alert them to social truths they would otherwise have been unwilling to accept. He forced his audience into a sort of double-take that must have delighted the dramatist within him.

The more closely the *Barbier* is examined, the more enjoyment is to be extracted from this concealed and subtle deliberation of purpose underlying every aspect of a play which appears upon casual inspection to be all froth and bubble.

The remarkable opening scenes, so brief and apparently so simple in their dramatic terms, in fact derive their impact from a bold use and blending of several theatrical traditions in such a way that, implicit within the beautifully woven pattern, is a parody of the very forms he draws upon.

It was inevitable that Beaumarchais, with all his natural ebullience gushing into his play and its central figure, should turn to *commedia dell'arte*, one of the most vital comedy forms in the whole history of the drama. From its popular uprising in sixteenth-century Italy, this specialised improvised comedy spread throughout all Europe, suffered many vicissitudes, enjoyed great triumph with royal and ducal patronage, and over the centuries evolved from an extremely coarse and often obscene slapstick into a sophisticated and polished art. Beaumarchais saw it in its decadence, for by the eighteenth century *commedia dell'arte* had become a bastard and dying form. Earlier in the century, the major troupe of Luigi Riccoboni, established in Paris, had shown what the genre could be. Riccoboni himself, known as Lelio since he played the lover, his Harlequin, Thomasso Antonio Vicenti, known as Thomassin, and the young Zanetta Benozzi, immortalised as the Silvia of Marivaux, were perhaps the last great players. After them, the Italian players increasingly performed in French plays, modifying their technique to meet new requirements, learning to perform in an alien tongue. They continued to improvise on a given scenario in the old manner from time to time, but the nature of the genre had changed and its unique power had gone from it.

In spite of Carlin, (Carlo Antonio Bertinazzi) the last of the great Harlequins, the Italian players were offering a degenerate form of their art when in 1765 they merged with the company of the Opéra Comique at the Hôtel de Bourgogne, scene of their former triumphs. Improvised comedy, as Beaumarchais knew it, had already absorbed many extraneous elements, and after the merger became still more involved with the genre evolved from the *théâtre de la foire*, and the fashionable *parades* which took over its Masks.

In the parallel development of all these theatre forms, spectacular presentations became increasingly fashionable, and the verbal element assumed greater importance: so *commedia dell'arte*, essentially a theatre of action and intrigue, changed fundamentally.

Beaumarchais made use of this debased and changed form, since it suited his purpose in a play where nothing is ever quite what it seems to be. Figaro apparently improvising a song, making up the words as he goes along, is in the Italian tradition and there is an aura of the Bergamasque valet about him: but his song has other values than the seeming ones, a sophistication of purpose unknown in the Italian genre. He is far less crude than Arlecchino, much more subtle than the most polished French Arlequin, far more intelligent, and even when he becomes the Count's valet he is of a higher social status. He is less poetic, less touching and sentimental than Thomassin, who incarnated the Arlequin of Marivaux's plays; gayer, surer of himself and of success than the melancholy Carlin. He is moreover, and this is of prime importance, liberated from the mask. He is himself; and by discarding the mask he has dissociated himself from the grotesque world of the Italian valet clowns, turned his crudely symbolic sword into a guitar, and achieved a human dignity that enables him to look his master in the eye, and establish his superiority over him.

He is at once in the long lineage of Italian clowns, which he comes near to closing; and apart from them.Without the mask, he is not forced to express himself in mime and gesture, to use his whole body to point a moment in the play. It is as though Arlecchino touched him on the shoulder and bestowed upon him, not an accolade, but the lithe movement, acrobatic control, and all the secret cunning developed over the centuries. In his infinite resource, his quick riposte, his activity upon his own and the Count's behalf he draws on the fertile invention of generations of the Italian *valets de comédie*; and transcends them all because he is outrageously himself, and they were always hidden behind their personas.

His slapstick is not physical, and this is perhaps symbolised by the change from stick or sword to guitar. He does not rely upon the *bastonnade* for humour, or for triumph over his adversaries, nor upon acrobatic tricks nor violent tumbling and chasing and fighting. In Figaro all these attributes of his forbears are transmuted: his acrobatics are verbal, his thrust and parry a brilliant gymnastic of the mind, capable of elaborating plot and counterplot. Words gush from him like spring waters, cascade in golden showers under the power of his enormous vitality.

The eighteenth-century audiences would have been aware of Figaro's progeniture and of his departure from it, his likeness and his difference. Many had seen, in their golden youth, the company Riccoboni brought to Paris. They would have enjoyed performances at the fair grounds of St. Germain and St. Laurent where the familiar Masks performed the same basic scenarii with an extraordinarily different technique, closer to that of the original acrobatic comedy. Moreover, these clowns, as if aware that their own kingdom was dying round them, had found a new and temporary lease of life in the *drame*, that somewhat plebeian form of drama geared to the newlyborn bourgeois class, presenting a social problem through types rather than characters—the Father, the Soldier, the Mother, the Young Girl,—an open invitation to the Masks; and in the *parades*, those highly indecent improvised private shows given by and for sophisticated degenerates who took great pleasure from their obscene licence. Some were based directly upon well-known Italian scenarii; in their lewd and pornographic content they went back to the earliest days of *commedia dell'arte*, but their presentation was elegant and intelligent: a perverse duality that brought infinite pleasure to high society, and to Beaumarchais. They were often given in a private language, comparable, at a high social level, to cockney rhyming or back slang, and this too derived in part from the incomprehensible jargon sometimes used by the clowns in earlier days. The Masks were present also in *opéra comique*, which was itself derived from a parody of grand opera invented by the *forains* in their long struggle against the monopoly of the Comédie Française.

All these dramatic forms were familiar to Beaumarchais' first audiences. What was not familiar was his use of them, the obliquity with which he suggested prototypes and then immediately withdrew the suggestion, an intellectual and dramatic titillation guaranteed to whet their jaded appetites.

The subject of the play, which recalls that of Molière's *Ecole des Femmes* and Regnard's *Folies amoureuses* is in itself a typical Italian scenario. Both E. Lintilhac and J. Scherer believe that the *Barbier* was first a *parade*, and most critics since have followed in this belief, though E. J. Arnould dissociates himself from it. It is certain that Beaumarchais had presented extremely successful *parades* privately at the Château d'Etioles where M. le Normand, husband of Mme de Pompadour, was host. It is certain that he very much enjoyed the genre, and was able to exercise his particular gift for parody within its framework. Yet there is undoubtedly more of the Italian scenario than of the *parade* in the *Barbier*, and the complexities of its construction give far more the illusion of an improvised comedy than of the perpetual parody necessary to the *parade*, though an element of parody runs throughout.

The mistake perhaps is to attempt to give pride of place to one form over another, to demonstrate an exact apportioning of elements.

For Beaumarchais in effect made the fullest use of a vast and complex theatrical tradition of comedy drawn from all available sources, ancient and modern, fashionable and unfashionable; and from a thousand shining threads tempered by time and usage he wove an intricate pattern in which each thread had its appointed place, and being in that place, contributed to a *trompe-l'œil* effect that has never before or since been equalled.

The *Barbier de Séville* owed much to contemporary comic opera. It was written originally for the Théâtre Italien, and presented as an *opéra bouffe*. Both E. Lintilhac, and more recently G. Bonneville in his popular edition of the play, have noted the several indications of this original version that have persisted in the final draft. There was in August 1964, a successful television performance of Pergolesi's *La Serva Padrona* which, for those who saw it, illumined these influences. The performance demonstrated the remarkable sense of timing, as did recent productions of Goldoni's plays; the entertaining blending of artificiality with naturalness, the gay *divertissement* belonging to the genre, of which Beaumarchais made such good use. He does not, as did Pergolesi and his peers, make his central character a woman. He had no interest in the threadbare theme of a pretty and intelligent woman achieving a successful marriage into a higher class: perhaps because Voltaire in *Nanine* disposed finally of a social prejudice that had already had its day. He created Figaro instead, the man Figaro; and from that moment political undertones and social significance of a wider order entered the gay golden world of comic opera.

It is significant that Madame Dussane, a leading actress of wide and diversified theatrical experience, playing at the Comédie Française, has recorded the fact that she never played Rosine in the *Mariage de Figaro* without feeling involved with her partner in a sort of stylised dance. She compared herself and her fellow players to ballet dancers perpetually on point, whose every movement must be carefully synchronised to meet the requirements of the breathtaking pace of the play. This analysis would be even more true of the *Barbier*, where perfect timing is even more essential; for here the repartees, soliloquies, dialogues, the verbal fencing, feints and ripostes; the overall pattern of movement, entrances and exits, juxtapositions, withdrawals, concealment, coincidences and concurrent action, are all part of a swift and fantastic counterpoint demanding the choreographic skill of a *guido mæstro* of exceptional experience and competence.

All is grist that comes to Beaumarchais' mill: the Franco-Spanish background, the heavily stressed Spanish atmosphere paradoxically creating one wholly French; the characters, costumes, plot and action drawn from Italian comedy; the philosophical and moralising bias lifted from the *drames*; verbal wit and paradox reminiscent of the *parades*; comic situations and incongruities stolen from the *farces*. Nothing is neglected, everything is made to serve, and in serving is transmuted through Beaumarchais' original approach to plots, techniques and characters that had become commonplace and decadent.

Critics have focussed attention upon what they believe to have been the purely literary sources of the play—Plautus; Sedaine, *On ne s'avise jamais de tout* (1761); Sallé, *Le Remède à la mode* (published 1881); Norland de Fatouville, *La Précaution inutile* (published 1717); Dorimond, *L'Ecole des Cocus, ou La Précaution inutile* (published 1661); Cailhava d'Estandoux, *Le Tuteur Dupé* (published 1765); Dancourt, *Les Vendanges de Suresne*[1] (published 1738), Marmontelle, *La Fausse Magie*; Molière, *L'Ecole des Femmes*, and Regnard *Les Folies amoureuses* (1704). Comparisons of this sort serve no very useful purpose, except to show how banal the subject of the play is, and how little Beaumarchais in fact owes to his predecessors. The subtitle of the play—*La Précaution inutile*—may, as Lintilhac points out, have been borrowed from Scarron, from whom Sedaine derived the title of his own *Gageure Imprévue* (1769), from which Beaumarchais took the basis of a scene for the *Mariage de Figaro*; but the same title occurs again in an operetta in one act by Achard (1760) as well as in some of the examples cited above. Similarly, the *Mémoires* of the Cardinal de Retz have been quoted as a source for the highly amusing scene in Act III, Scene 11 when the conspirators Figaro, the Count and Rosine, are on tenterhooks that either Bartholo or Don Bazile or both will reveal to each other the different deceptions in which they have been involved, while the two old men try vainly to understand the innuendoes and heavily veiled hints each offers the other. Comparison with Molière is inevitable, since both playwrights seek to provoke laughter, but the nature and quality of the laughter is different. There are obvious similarities of plot between *L'Ecole des Femmes* and *Le Barbier de Séville*, and both bear the same subtitle—*ou La Précaution inutile*. The

[1] A short *farce* played *en travesti* in which a young girl is carried off in spite of her guardian. It was billed with *Le Barbier de Séville* at its first performance.

significance of this fact, however, can easily be overstressed, since it was common practice in both centuries to take existing farces, comedies, stories and *commedia dell'arte* scenarii, bestowing familiar and extant titles upon the several different versions achieved by different hands.

The plot common to both the aforementioned comedies is already to be found in Scarron's *nouvelle*, *La Précaution inutile*, an adaptation of *El Prevenido Engañado* by one Doña Maria de Zayas y Sotomayor; in a translation of a sixteenth-century Italian *novella* to be found under the title *Les Facétieuses Nuits* in Straparola's collection; and maybe in an Italian scenario, many of which sketched similar plots to be improvised by the players. Yet it is not so much the similarities of plot and character that are interesting as their divergences, due in part no doubt to the passing of time, but mostly to the distinctive creative gifts of Molière and Beaumarchais. There is a noticeable difference in the pace, structure and style brought to bear upon the similar plot, in the conception and implementation of the comedy line. Molière shared the theatre of the Palais Royal from 1660 with the Italian troup led by the Arlequin Locatelli, and was profoundly influenced by their specialised comedy form. *L'Ecole des Femmes* was first performed in 1662, and is far closer to Italian comedy in its characters, its presentation, and its *jeu de scène* than is *Le Barbier*. *L'Ecole des Femmes* is in effect an Italian scenario transformed and elevated into a superb comedy by the particular dramatic genius of Molière. *Le Barbier* is as swift in pace, as excellent in structure; but Beaumarchais makes oblique and subtle use of certain aspects of *commedia dell'arte*, as he does of diverse and traditional comedy forms, and gives the ancient *commedia* characters a new and contemporary look. Agnès and Arnolphe are stereotypes of Isabella and Pantalone enlivened by Molière's wit and power; Rosine and Bartholo have taken a longer and more complicated journey away from their prototypes, and come to represent far more than the ingénue and her old doddering guardian and would-be groom. *L'Ecole des Femmes* is in Molière's flexible verse, with scope allowed for excellent tirades; while *Le Barbier* is in equally flexible prose, related to the easy flow of Beaumarchais' language and the action of his comedy, and seen by its author as a necessary part of the ease of his play: 'En écrivant mes pièces' he wrote in *Notes et Réfléxions* 'j'ai préféré une prose harmonieuse à la coupe et à la césure des vers.'

Beaumarchais was able to convey that deep sense of freedom which is the essence of comedy, and which, indeed, in farce becomes anarchy. This essential freedom was already present in Molière's plays; and for both dramatists it was symbolized and expressed in the servant-master relationship prevalent in all Italian comedy, from its early farcical—and anarchic—presentation, in which Arlecchino and Brighella confused and confounded all the projects of their masters with the best will in the world, and were beaten for their pains, through all the vicissitudes of the developing genre until, in Molière's hands, the paradox of a valet wittier and cleverer than his master began clearly to emerge. Then, with Beaumarchais, the servant was so clearly superior in every respect to his distinguished master that he constitutes in the end a social and political danger. When Beaumarchais wrote 'Toute croyance à la fatalité dégrade l'homme en lui ôtant la liberté, hors laquelle il n'y a nulle moralité dans ses actions,' he was expressing a view which Molière would have shared.

Yet it would be unwise to argue that Beaumarchais was greatly influenced by Molière; for he was in fact open to all influences without being greatly affected by any. Le Barbier bears witness to the fact that he drew upon multiple sources and took from them whatever he required, without apparent preference for any specific comedy form or any specific author or playwright. Lintilhac has listed all cases in which Molière uses travesti as a theatrical device. All these exercises have little specific value, since it was customary for playwrights to draw freely upon existing or previously used plots, situations and characters. They do, however serve to demonstrate that Beaumarchais, through his exuberant creative force, transformed banal scenarii and traditional plays, filched from all the diverse elements of French and Italian comedy, into an original work as viable today as in its own time. Herein lies the true comparison with Molière of the previous century, and with Regnard and Marivaux in his own, though other less general ones may successfully be made. Claude Roy in his lively book Lire Marivaux has demonstrated the close relationship between Trivelin and Figaro, revealed in the following passage from Act I scene 1 of La Fausse Suivante of Marivaux:

'Depuis quinze ans que je roule dans le monde, tu sais combien je me suis tourmenté, combien j'ai fait d'efforts pour arriver à un état fixe. J'avais entendu dire que les scrupules nuisaient à la fortune; je fis trêve avec les miens, pour n'avoir rien à me reprocher. Était-il question d'avoir de l'honneur? j'en avais. Fallait-il être fourbe? j'en soupirais, mais j'allais mon train. Je me suis vu quelquefois à mon aise; mais le moyen d'y rester avec le jeu, le vin et les femmes? Comment se mettre à l'abri de ces fléaux-là?...

'Que te dirai-je enfin? Tantôt maître, tantôt valet; toujours prudent, toujours industrieux; ami des fripons par intérêt, ami des honnêtes gens par goût; traité poliment sous une figure, menacé d'étrivières sous une

autre; changeant à propos de métier, d'habit, de caractère, de mœurs;
risquant beaucoup, résistant peu; libertin dans le fond, réglé dans la
forme; démasqué par les uns, soupçonné par les autres, a la fin équivoque
à tout le monde, j'ai tâté de tout; je dois partout; mes créanciers sont de
deux espèces: les uns ne savent pas que je leur dois; les autres le savent et
le sauront longtemps. J'ai logé partout, sur le pavé, chez l'aubergiste, au
cabaret, chez le bourgeois, chez l'homme de qualité, chez moi, chez la
justice, qui m'a souvent recueilli dans mes malheurs; mais ses apparte-
ments sont trop tristes, et je n'y faisais que des retraites; enfin, mon ami,
après quinze ans de soins, de travaux et de peines, ce malheureux paquet
est tout ce qui me reste; voilà ce que le monde m'a laissé, l'ingrat!
après ce que j'ai fait pour lui! tous ses présents, pas une pistole.'

It is Trivelin who speaks, but it could easily be the voice of Figaro, and
particularly the Figaro of *Le Mariage*. This speech from Marivaux's play
presages the Figaro of the *Mariage* in style as well as in content, but it can
also be linked with Figaro's speech in Act I scene 2 of the *Barbier*. Claude
Roy goes so far as to call *La Fausse Suivante* Beaumarchais' first comedy.
Certainly, in the long series of *valets de comédie* this Trivelin stands out as a
landmark, since he is marked by the delicate ingenuity of Marivaux, and
so still further removed from the earlier buffoons from whom he is
directly derived. But this similarity of speech and situation between
Trivelin and Figaro is interesting rather than deeply significant. The
tenor and meaning of Marivaux's play, and his conception of theatre are
different. Like Molière, Marivaux adhered more closely to the pattern
and principles of Italian comedy and its presentation by one specific
company than did Beaumarchais. In his theatre, he delved more deeply
into the secret recesses of the human heart. Trivelin is a valet of secondary
importance beside the mightiest of his line; but Marivaux's prime interest
and therefore that of his audiences is focussed upon the awakening of love
in Silvia's young and untried heart. Even in the *Jeu de l'Amour et du
Hasard*, the fine and pointed clowning, the vagaries of valet and soubrette,
are still subordinated to the exquisite love-game played out between
master and mistress and duplicated by servant and maid. This is a basic
difference between the comedies of Marivaux and those of Beaumarchais, where Figaro is king and love has several faces.

'Il paraît qu'il ne lui fallait pas moins qu'un procès criminel pour déve-
lopper tous ses talents pour le genre comique', wrote a critic in the
Correspondance littéraire of December 1773, even more truly than he

knew. Before that date, Pierre-Augustin Caron the clockmaker, transformed into Caron de Beaumarchais by the simple process of assuming the name of his first wife's estate near Arpajon, and acquiring the patronage of the King's mistress Madame de Pompadour, was happily engaged in climbing the social ladder with speed and energy, making money and influential friends, and taking full advantage of his entrée at Court and in high society.

He had always been a theatre lover, and now, with time and money to spare, and the assurance of a well disposed audience, he amused himself, writing verse and playlets for private performances. His interest soon centred upon the *drame*, a new form of theatre promoted by Diderot, which aimed at introducing reality into the theatre. Classical or legendary themes were to be abandoned in favour of those dealing with ordinary men and women, set in contemporary social conditions, expressing normal feeling in everyday speech; and there was, among the most earnest of the partisans of this new form, a desire to abolish the rigid distinction between comedy and tragedy in favour of a more flexible emotional content. The *drame*, referred to by its supporters as serious or bourgeois drama, by its detractors as sentimental or drivelling, and by its arch-opponent Voltaire as 'comédie horrible', inspired Beaumarchais to write his first real play *Eugénie ou la Vertu malheureuse*. Written for the Théâtre Français, it was a complete failure upon its first presentation. In two days, Beaumarchais rewrote and reshaped it, reducing the five acts to four; and in this revised form it enjoyed a moderate success. Three years later he presented his second *drame*, *Les Deux Amis ou le Négociant de Lyon*, a failure so catastrophic that this time even Beaumarchais admitted defeat by not attempting to rewrite or to present it again.

When *Eugénie* was published in the same year of its presentation, the author added as preface an *Essai sur le Genre dramatique sérieux* (1767), in which he expressed his attitude to the theatre and his intentions as a playwright. It is not unexpected that Beaumarchais, an artisan's son accepted at Court, should be interested in bourgeois drama, nor, keen litigant, that he should be aware of its function as a means of expressing anti-clericalism on a safe platform: a lay pulpit that had not hitherto existed, and which made the form popular in its own day, when the middle classes were for the first time achieving power and prestige. With a taste for adventure and for novelty, he was bound to plunge into the fray and announce himself an ardent supporter of the *drame*. Even after the partial failure of *Eugénie* and the total failure of *Les Deux Amis*,

Beaumarchais remained attached to the form, with a nostalgia that betrayed itself in the moral and sentimental soliloquies and commentaries he interpolated in his comedies, and which were subsequently cut, either by himself, or by the actors who played in them.

Examined from this angle, both *Le Barbier de Séville* and *Le Mariage de Figaro* are astonishing digressions from his theatre aesthetic, as laid down in the *Essai sur le Genre dramatique sérieux*, and as more normally practised by him. Moreover, twenty years later, he returned to a form closely approaching the *drame* with *La Mère coupable* (1792). It is so different in form and content from *Le Barbier* and *Le Mariage* that the only claim it can make to forming a trilogy with these lies in the fact that the same characters appear in it at a later stage in their lives, and without their former vitality.

It would be foolish to suppose that the lack of success attending the performance of his two *drames* turned Beaumarchais from his avowed intent in the theatre; for his attachment to that specific form of drama demonstrably lasted all his life. There were other and stronger reasons for his digression.

III

It is typically ironic that the years 1770-1777, described in a letter to Madame Panckoucke (November 22nd 1779) as 'les sept ou huit années qui ont empoisonné mon âge viril', led to the creation of his masterpiece, and his assured place in the immortality of literature. To seek to understand this implicit paradox is to plunge into a series of extraordinary events, subtly blending comedy with tragedy, a sequence of fantastic adventures as lively as any to be found in the picaresque novels of the time, and as fast and furious as the pace of the comedy resulting from them.

It began with the death of the great financier Pâris-Duverney in 1770. Several years before, Beaumarchais had been instrumental in restoring him to favour at Court, as a result of which Pâris-Duverney became his patron and benefactor, making him an allowance, helping his career by securing for him appointments as secretary to the King and magistrate to put down poaching on royal preserves, and keeping him abreast of safe speculation in the money markets. Through him, Beaumarchais climbed still higher up the social ladder, making a fortune as well as influential friends at Court and in the world of big business; and upon his death Beaumarchais was still protected by a deed drawn up three months before, leaving him a considerable sum of money and other property. Count Falcoz de la Blache, the heir, immediately repudiated the deed, and accused Beaumarchais of forging Pâris-Duverney's signature to it. Two years later, Beaumarchais won his case before the tribunal to whom he had submitted it, and La Blache immediately lodged an appeal. Beaumarchais meanwhile had turned his attention to his own work, and finished an *opéra-comique*, *Le Barbier de Séville*, written for the Italian Comedians, who refused it. He then turned it into a comedy, and in 1773 it was accepted by the Comédie Française, who announced a forthcoming production in February, since Marin, the censor had passed it for public performance.

It was then that Beaumarchais became involved in an explosive love triangle. He had been enjoying the favours of one Mademoiselle Ménard, an Italian player under the protection of the violent and tempestuous Duc de Chaulnes. A discarded mistress betrayed the lovers to him, and the noble Duke descended upon Beaumarchais with every intention of despatching him from this earth. The battle was so prolonged and inconclusive that the King clapped de Chaulnes into jail at Vincennes, to bring an end to the scandalous affair. Beaumarchais incautiously celebrated his triumph over a peer of the realm in a witty and satiric *mémoire*, and was himself thrown into jail at Fort-L'Evèque, known as the Actor's Bastille, to be held there until May 8th. As a result of this, the first performance of the *Barbier* was postponed; and Beaumarchais had time to realise that the hearing of La Blache's appeal against the verdict given in his own favour was due to be heard on April 5th, while he himself was still in prison.

Since he was required by law to present his case to the presiding magistrate, on this occasion Goëzman, an Alsatian, he obtained permission to leave prison on necessary business. To no avail: La Blache had already suborned Goëzman, so that when Beaumarchais applied twice to meet him in February and March, he was twice refused. On April 1st Goëzman was officially declared in charge, and three times on that day Beaumarchais tried to see him, and failed to do so. In the following two days, he tried six times, without success. His family and friends then met with the Magistrate's wife, and bargained with her to secure the necessary interview, to which she graciously consented upon receipt of two hundred louis, a watch mounted in diamonds, and fifteen additional louis to share with the judge's secretary. Two days later Goëzman decided in favour of La Blache, who immediately sent bailiffs to distrain Beaumarchais' goods. During the six years in which the La Blache affair dragged on in a series of extraordinary and unbelievable complications, Beaumarchais was never brought nearer to bankruptcy and social ruin than he was at this moment, with his case lost, the inheritance from Duverney denied him, his goods impounded, and himself imprisoned.

Yet there were consolations. The palpably unjust verdict had aroused great anger and added to the unpopularity of the notoriously corrupt *parlement* Maupeou, to which Goëzman and his colleagues belonged, under the auspices of the Duc d'Aiguillon, le Chancelier Maupeou and the Abbé Terray, and imposed upon *parlement* by the King, Louis XV. It was finally the Duc de la Vrillière who unconsciously lit the firework of Beaumarchais' comic verve. It was the Duke himself who had been responsible for throwing Beaumarchais into prison; it was the Duke who recognised the danger signals of public anger and dissatisfaction, the hostility to the *parlement* Maupeou; and he who advised Beaumarchais, released from prison on May 5th, not to show his face in public, but to go away quietly into the country.

Unfortunately for him, and for all associated with him, Beaumarchais' natural resilience was already at work, and his reply to this suggestion was twofold—a formal letter of thanks, and a witty and amusing *mémoire*. written for his own pleasure and widely circulated among his friends At the same time, Madame Goëzman, for fear of still greater scandal, was forced to return the two hundred louis and the diamond-studded watch she had received as 'presents'! But she was so determined to keep at least part of her ill-gotten gains that she found herself unable to return the fifteen louis: she had already given them to her husband's secretary, who promptly denied having received them. It is a pleasing thought, considering the whole unsavoury affair, that in effect these fifteen louis eventually brought down the *parlement* Maupeou, released hitherto unsuspected talent in Beaumarchais and in the end served to give back to him all that he had lost.

Goëzman, alarmed at the turn taken in his affairs by the discovery of his wife's lying and its repercussions, and shaken no doubt by a pun going the rounds in Paris—'Louis quinze a détruit le parlement ancien et quinze louis détruiront le nouveau'—decided that the best form of defence was attack. Secure in the protection of the Duc d'Aiguillon, one of the all powerful triumvirate, Goëzman served a writ on Beaumarchais for attempting to bribe a magistrate, so that the latter found himself involved in another court case, this time before the Criminal Court.

It is evident that Beaumarchais was not cast down by the troubles that beset him; for while the case dragged on, he wrote and published the four *Mémoires* against Goëzman that, in the opinion of Voltaire, were masterpieces of polemic writing second only to the *Lettres Provinciales* of Pascal. In them, he drew upon his gifts of lucidity, volubility, and sheer comic exuberance to establish himself for all time as a brilliant polemist and consummate dialectician, and more than able to make his own case one of general significance.

The Goëzman affair lasted a year, but its repercussions were enormous, only some of which concern us here. In February 1774 both Goëzman and his wife were condemned, and the former deprived of his magistrature. But Beaumarchais' vindication turned out to be moral rather than legal, since he too was condemned to forfeit his magistrature and other civic rights, so that the case left him bankrupt and without a career, or so it seemed.

Yet in Beaumarchais' life, as in his greatest play, nothing is ever what it seems. During this tempestuous year, he had not only found in the *Mémoires* his true identity as a writer, but he had continued to concern himself with the *Barbier*. He gave readings to his friends on several occasions; and both he and the Comédie Française discovered that there was an increasing demand for it among the general public. It was reported that Beaumarchais had incorporated within its framework references to his jousting with the law and with authority. And a public that had avidly followed the La Blache and Goëzman affairs, chuckled over the amorous tangle with the Duc de Chaulnes, been titillated by the brilliantly comic *Mémoires*, and were ready and eager to cry down the corrupt *parlement* Maupeou, felt cheated of the promised performance of the play.

Beaumarchais, whose eye was always on the public, however involved he became with his complicated affairs, had in fact revised and altered the text that he had presented to the Comédie Française, and had added allusions to the events and the persons that had filled his mind during this crowded year. Don Bazile for example acquired some of the characteristics of Marin, who had censored and passed the play for performance in 1772, and then retracted permission following the de Chaulnes affair, including a Provençal accent and turn of speech. In other versions, Don Bazile was called Guzman or Colmaro (Goëzman came from Colmar), and both he and Bartholo showed resemblances here and there to the Alsacian. There were also wisecracks, innuendoes and, later, interpolated speeches and commentaries referring to the several affairs in which Beaumarchais had been involved. Yet this was not simply opportunism. It was also the result of a double liberation that had taken place as a consequence of these events.

As the critic of the *Correspondance littéraire* had so sapiently pointed out, the *Mémoires* released Beaumarchais' great gift for comedy, in their content, their purpose, and their presentation. Side by side with this, the litigation at so many different levels during this most decisive year of his life, sharpened his natural talents and exercised the technical power of a born dramatist. For the Law is drama in its purest essence, its processes are as ritualistic as the origins of theatre, the law courts are a natural theatre: the plot is set down in black and white, the antagonists are in absolute opposition, and the rest of the personnel in support of one side or the other. The law is moreover so often unconsciously comic that Beaumarchais not only moved in an arena expressly fashioned to fit his special genius, but one in which his comic verve could find the fullest expression; and this at a moment when any other man would have been pulled down by his financial ruin and loss of civic dignity. In the event these factors, interwoven with the already involved genres drawn upon by Beaumarchais, added to the originality of the play; and though at first his natural exuberance, allied to the sense of liberation, and his awareness of popular support led him into excesses, in due course the balance was redressed, and the play emerged in its final form.

While it was still in what turned out to be an interim stage, and with minor revisions insisted upon, it was approved by the Censor Arthaud who had replaced Marin, its performance authorized by the Chief of Police de Sartines, and rehearsals were immediately set in train for a performance to take place on February 12th 1774, which was cancelled on February 10th as a result of the machinations of his old enemies the Duc d'Aiguillon and the Duc de la Vrillière. This setback, followed by the greater one of the verdict in the Goëzman case, led Beaumarchais to hand over the manuscript of the *Barbier* to his unfailing friend and patron the Prince de Conti, and to plunge into his well-known adventures as secret agent, largely self-appointed, of the King, in an attempt to rehabilitate himself at Court and in Society. As the James Bond of eighteenth-century France, he travelled to England, where he acquired enough English to bestow the rudiments of the language upon Figaro at a later date; to Holland, Austria, and once more to England, on fantastic missions that, successfully concluded, brought him back into favour at Court, reconciled him with the Duc d'Aiguillon and Madame Du Barry, and brought him into contact with the Chevalier d'Eon, that ambiguous character, and with Lord Mayor Wilkes and other adherents to the cause of the American rebels into which Beaumarchais plunged wholeheartedly, taking France with him. His restoration to royal favour enabled him once more to seek permission to show the *Barbier*.

At the end of 1774 the unpopular *parlement* Maupeou, which had lasted for three years, was abolished by the newly reigning monarch Louis XVIth, and Beaumarchais immediately rushed to demand justice against the infamous sentence passed upon him. It took a further two years to clear his name, a delay due to the fact that Beaumarchais refused to accept the form of pardon offered, and demanded a total and royal recantation of the sentence. But already, a year earlier, he found himself re-established at Court and in government circles; and the *Barbier* passed the censor, this time Crébillon *fils*, for the third time, and achieved its first performance on February 23rd 1775.

In spite of an excellent cast, this long-awaited première was a disaster. In the interim period since the play had been accepted by the Comédie Française early in 1773, Beaumarchais had misjudged a situation that had changed fundamentally. In the beginning, the Goëzman affair was topical and the public excited by the case and its repercussions, and delighted with the *Mémoires*: Beaumarchais enjoyed the sympathy and support of the people during his several vicissitudes. In order therefore to assure the success of his comedy, and also no doubt because he was wholly absorbed in his litigious games with authority, he loaded the play with personal polemics, gross allusions to the Goëzman affair, digressions, interpolations, a heavy and vulgar humour, and extended it from four acts to five: so that it became too long and intensely boring. The characters became the mouthpiece of Beaumarchais in an undisciplined way, and so had no vitality, nor depth, while the plot caved in under the load and became of no consequence whatever. This first version performed was totally non-selective, a diatribe loosely expressed in stage terms, and therefore without artistry or creative discipline.

Moreover, it came at the wrong time. Topics of the day have a habit of becoming tomorrow's dead horse, and nothing will flog it into life again. The public had for a long time been titillated by the thought of Beaumarchais' play. In 1774, it was eagerly awaited by those expecting the brilliant fireworks and scandalous frankness of the *Mémoires*, who hoped for an attack on the *parlement* Maupeou, and the revelation of corruption in high places. But by 1775, the fickle mob were no longer interested in the Goëzman affair, had half forgotten Beaumarchais and his picaresque adventures in law, while the *parlement* Maupeou had been dissolved by royal decree; and the topicality and public excitement for which Beaumarchais sacrificed his original version in fact no longer existed. Rather like Anne Boleyn's eventual marriage to Henry VIII, the waiting time had been too long, and the affair was already sour at the roots and doomed to failure.

Nothing ever pleased Beaumarchais as much as a good fight; nor did he ever accept defeat. His extraordinary natural resilience, which he bestowed upon Figaro, enabled him to recover from near mortal blows with astonishing rapidity. In this case he apparently repeated the pattern of eight years before, when he rewrote *Eugénie* in no time at all, following the failure of its first presentation. Three days after the disastrous opening of the *Barbier*, a revised form in four acts was put upon the stage by the same company; and friends and critics alike marvelled at the speed and genius with which an unwieldy, badly constructed play, boring and over long, was transformed into a taut swiftly-flowing sparkling comedy, with original characters and an ebullient charm.

Yet the explanation, as both E. J. Arnould and E. Lintilhac have pointed out, is not so much miraculous as obvious. Beaumarchais went back to the original version, known to the actors for two years, and twice at least put into rehearsal for performances that were then cancelled; and with certain emendations, the wholly successful production was given its final rehearsal and set before a public that recognized with delight the hand that had written the *Mémoires*. That delight has been shared through the centuries that have passed since then, from the first presentation before the Court at Versailles, by the Queen's command, until the present day.

Beaumarchais' fame spread abroad. The play was translated into English, a German adaptation was made, and musical formis that are legion—ballets, pantomimes, operas and *opéra-bouffes*, in particular those of Païsiello (1780) and of Rossini (1816), with libretti growing ever further from Beaumarchais' original play. Indeed the magic of the *Barbier* is such that even though Rossini's opera seemed to have ousted

Païsiello's, there have nevertheless been three revivals of the latter in recent years: in Milan by the Piccolo Scala, in Berlin by the Komische Oper, and in Rome by the Piccolo Teatro Musicali. This last production, mounted by Corrado Pavolini, was presented also, towards the end of 1965 at Montreux, prior to going to Russia. The two Italian and the German versions varied a great deal as to elements stressed, the projection of comedy and the placing of emphasis: but one thing shone from all three and that was the indestructibility of the ebullient Figaro, towering above all others in whatsoever alien tongue.

In his own time, Beaumarchais was able to note that the *Barbier* was performed 118 times at the Comédie Française, up to the closing of the theatre in 1792; and by 1962, the total of performances given had reached 1098.

But perhaps the real triumph for Beaumarchais, the clockmaker's son, was the performance that was put on at court in 1785, with Marie-Antoinette herself playing Rosine, and the Comte d'Artois taking the part of the Barber. This must have brought great pleasure to the man who was determined to climb the social ladder, having first taken the precaution of ennobling his own name. One feels that that particular performance even outweighed the glory of the year 1778, in which he finally won his case against La Blache, after eight years of struggle, so triumphantly that La Blache was not only compelled to honour all the terms of Duverney's bequests but also to offer compensation to the man he had hounded so ruthlessly. Beaumarchais found himself at last in the possession of his fortune, with his full civic rights and his office as magistrate restored to him.

It has been stated that the miracle of the entire reshaping of the *Barbier* in the three days between its first and second showing has a simple explanation; there is however no simple explanation of the miracle of the comedy itself.

E. J. Arnould, in his recent major study *La Genèse du Barbier de Séville* (1965), reproduces the text of the five-act version, together with the principal variants to be discovered in the three other extant manuscripts and in the text of the first published edition of the play in four acts, which, with certain corrections and deletions, marked a return to the earlier manuscripts. The text of this first published edition was the one played in 1775, and has served as a model for all subsequent editions and productions.

The play in five acts, presented only once, on February 23rd 1775, bears witness to Beaumarchais' activities during the two years he struggled to put it on stage, in the reference to Figaro's diplomatic missions abroad, his jaunty awareness of the mainspring of the English tongue, and his abortive authorship; in the brilliant digression on calumny, delivered by Bazile and incorporated into the definitive version; and the vicious portrait of Bartholo which contains certain of Goëzman's less attractive physical characteristics—'qui tousse et crache et geint tour à tour'—and his well known squint translated into a crippled arm.

Beaumarchais' preoccupation with the imbroglios that bedevilled his existence led him to burden his earlier lighthearted comedy with sour comment, heavy humour in somewhat poor taste, and several digressions of varying length whenever the spirit moved him or some passage in the earlier version gave him scope. Inevitably the pace of the comedy was slowed down, the content clogged, and its humour reduced. It is not surprising that the play in this form should have failed with an audience waiting expectantly for the wit and sparkle they associated with the author of the *Mémoires*. Nor is it surprising that Beaumarchais was determined to wrest success from his failure, for that was the pattern set throughout his life.

The success was absolute. The comedy, in its final form, offered something to theatregoers of all tastes and all political opinions; and everything to the intelligent élite. Exception must be made for the actor who considered himself insulted when the leading rôle in Beaumarchais' comedy was offered to him. He was in fact the son of a barber, and clearly, would prefer to play the Count, blinded as he was by his own class-consciousness to the real balance of power in the play.

An examination of the four manuscripts extant serves to show by what deft and certain touches the somewhat undisciplined and self-indulgent five-act version was transformed into a masterpiece drawn largely from earlier versions, and polished and manipulated by a writer now in possession of his full powers. All the processes of creative work are there displayed. His literary hesitation is shown by the transposition, for example, of Scene 6 in Act I of the earlier manuscript to Act II Scene 8 in the final version; or by his division of the earlier Act III into Acts III and IV for the five act version, in an attempt to redress the balance of a version grown unwieldy. Throughout there are multiple small modifications, due in part to his determination to pull off a success, and to his awareness of the changed taste and reaction of the public; but mostly to his own increased mastery and technical skill.

The major changes that occur are those between the earlier four act version and the five-act one which proved disastrous. Most of the personal passages that were added, much of the polemic that stemmed from his lawsuits and that reflected his chequered career in the years between and his treatment at the hands of corrupt politicians, disappear from the final draft. He turns back to his earlier version, and with minor emendations and transpositions is able to turn personal into general polemic, woven into the texture of the play, which ceases to be the personal apologia of Beaumarchais, and becomes once more a comedy concerning a certain barber of Seville. It is clear that the actors were more at ease during the second performance; and this is certainly due to the fact that they were playing in a version much more familiar to them than the one of the first performance.

The slight but significant modifications shown between the early and the final four act version bring about significant improvements as though, having passed through the crucible of the five-act comedy, it had become pure gold. Growing importance is attached to the structure of the play, the smooth disclosure of its plot, and to its general dramatic quality. With every modification, every deletion, every transposition, the swift flowing scenes are more rigorously linked together in an increasingly flexible and masterly shape.

Certain elements that seemed most destructive in the five-act version, serve in their proper place to add to the originality of the play. Beaumarchais' experiences in law, in society, as a secret agent, and as a dramatist had been traumatic during those years in which the *Barbier* was evolving through its several forms. The personal element, introduced into the five-act version regardless of artistic requirements, pared down, absorbed, changed into general commentary on the nature of mankind and the social pattern of the time, in line with the earlier version, still contains traces of Beaumarchais' dilemma, and mingles the essence of the suffering man with that of the somewhat younger and much happier Beaumarchais who wrote the original version. This adds a new note at a time when playwrights were more concerned with the moral or philosophical aspects of life than they were with polemics or personal intervention.

Beaumarchais became an innovator in another sense, and equally by accident. Having extended his comedy to five acts, it would have been impossible, without serious loss of form and content to compress it into the more usual three act comedy. It would be difficult to find another great four act comedy in the history of the theatre. Comedy being granted certain freedoms from normal requirements in drama, it was common to find one or three act plays in that genre; but a four-act comedy was a *tour de force*, and Beaumarchais' own commentary on it is typical:

> ... ma pièce est restée en cinq actes, qui sont le premier, le deuxième, le troisième au théâtre, le quatrième au diable, et le cinquième avec les trois premiers. Tel auteur vous soutiendra que ce quatrième acte, qu'on n'y voit point, n'en est pas moins celui qui fait le plus de bien à la pièce en ce que l'on ne l'y voit point. Laissons jaser le monde; il me suffit d'avoir prouvé mon dire; il me suffit en faisant mes cinq actes d'avoir montré mon respect pour Aristote, Aubignac, et les Modernes, et d'avoir mis ainsi l'honneur de la règle à couvert. Par le second arrangement le diable a son affaire; mon char n'en roule pas moins bien sans la cinquième roue; le public est content, je le suis aussi.[1]

As usual, Beaumarchais had made the best of both worlds. While in practice remaining close to the accepted basic form for comedy, he had nevertheless shown signs of a certain disrespect for convention, and of freedom from dramatic prejudice. These are perhaps the smallest manifestation of his freedom, but they are symbolic of the winds of change blowing from every quarter, that were made manifest in Figaro himself.

IV

The plot of his comedy was excellently well summarized by Beaumarchais himself:

'Un vieillard amoureux prétend épouser demain sa pupille; un jeune amant plus adroit le prévient; et ce jour même en fait sa femme, à la barbe et dans la maison du tuteur'.[2]

In fact, this is the well-worn plot of a thousand Italian scenarii, taken and used by French dramatists in multiple comedies since the Italian

---

[1] *Lettre modérée*, ed. Arnould: p. 497.
[2] *Op. cit.*, p. 493.

Masks first trod the boards: yet, transformed by Beaumarchais' particular genius as it had earlier been transformed by Molière, and in his own century by Marivaux, the same basic plot was used as the core of totally different masterpieces of the French theatre.

In this case, one of the new elements is the fantastic speed with which the plot is expounded, developed, and brought to its climax. The play contains forty four scenes, as against, for example, the twenty one of Molière's *Le Misanthrope*, and so closely linked and so superbly integrated that they move like the surge of a sunlit sea. The early scenes give the swift presentation of all the key elements of the play, unfold the plot, and introduce all the characters, with well-established personalities at once belonging to the old traditions and breaking away from them. They contain moreover a careful preparation for future scenes, and the special data given is so timed that the spectator is always slightly better informed than the characters involved, so that his enjoyment of the imbroglio is increased by his prescience. Nor does this foreknowledge in any way destroy the tension and the surprise element: partly because they are sustained and carried along by the flow of the close-knit scenes; partly because of the several contrivances, no doubt drawn from the *lazzi* of the Italian Arlecchino, by which the inventive genius of Figaro is deployed to counter the skilful moves of his worthy opponent Bartholo; lastly because not all of these contrivances are successful, and therefore alter the predicted course of events, as in Act III Scene 3, where the movements of perplexity are cleverly handled and extremely funny to watch. In Act II the plot thickens, and so many complications are introduced that it seems Beaumarchais must have taken extreme pleasure in his masterly juggling of persons and events, as for example in Scenes 9 and 14. There is perhaps only one scene, Act II Scene 4, which is not strictly necessary to the action, but most critics and all but the most curmudgeonly spectators, now as in the past agree that it is most effective on stage, with its eight 'répliques' punctuated by the single word 'Monsieur', which M. Scherer likened to 'une sorte de chant amébée utilisé pour l'injure ou de stichomythie assouplie par l'emploi de la prose.'[1]

One reason for the speed with which the play proceeds is the fact that throughout there are only two simple sets: the scene changes from the street scene of Act I with its row of houses with barred windows, in one of which live Bartholo and Rosine, to an interior of Rosine's

---

[1] *La Dramaturgie de Beaumarchais*, p. 118.

room with the barred window still dominating the set, but seen this time from the inside; and back again, according to the requirements of the play, without any interference of course from the opening or closing of curtains. This simplicity of décor enables the scenes to pass from one to the other, and the acts to follow on with exceptional ease and speed.

There are curious side effects here, as there are throughout the play. The pace gives the work as a whole the impression of being not only a parody of life, but a travesty of Italian comedy, where so much depended on exact and skilful timing, rather as an old film shown on a modern projector is speeded up and becomes twice as funny. Paradoxically, it adds verisimilitude, in the oblique sense that no one has time to reflect on the gratuitous nature of many of the events or question their source. In a sense, the audience mount upon a merry-go-round and are dazed into acquiescence through the speed with which it turns. It all became a great game of battledore and shuttlecock, with the spectators as breathless participants in the match.

Even the dialogue of the play becomes a factor in its speed, a dazzling counterpoint to the rhythm and harmony of the swift moving scenes. Crisp staccato interchange, filled with word play and an exuberance of language, ideas and commentary on specific events or general attitudes to life and love, offer a varied tempo of speech and a rhythmic pattern of verbal dexterity equal to that shown in the construction of the play: so much so that the dialogue of this comedy may well be considered an integral part of the structure of the play, in a manner that was never true before or since until Ionesco and Beckett, in this present century and in their different ways, made similar structural use of verbal manipulation and the rhythms of speech.

In the first four scenes of the play, elements of exposition are woven into the fabric of the dialogue in interchanges between characters recently or newly met, or in soliloquies interspersed with deft asides of a moral or philosophical nature. These asides, which fall naturally into place wherever they are spoken, serve to divert the spectator from the realisation that he is being introduced to a plot and those who will sustain it. This exposition is exceptionally subtle and successful, written with an expertness that acquaints the audience with the inner feelings, past history, present position and future plans of the characters concerned, without any impediment to the rapidity with which the plot is unfolded and the action engaged. Beaumarchais' inventiveness is such that this necessary exposition, so often a tedious element in the plays of the period, becomes in his hands another source of wit and humour, and a revelation of the ambiguous nature of everything that is happening on stage.

Beaumarchais is equally resourceful linguistically, and his dialogue, like his play, is unique, paradoxically because of the many elements he draws from diverse sources. His style is humorous, witty, gay, aphoristic, laconic, eloquent, petulant, Rabelaisian or moral, according to the nature of the characters and the requirements of the plot. Some of his couplets are derived from the original version he wrote in 1772 as an *opéra comique* for the Italian players. There are bravura set-pieces like Bazile's speech on calumny (Act II Scene 8), and cascades of verbal fireworks, as in Figaro's masterly summing up of the reasons for which he left Madrid (Act I Scene 3). There is a strong musical influence in the style of the play, with pianissimo and crescendo passages, and masterpieces of *phrases accumulatives*.

The exuberant vitality of the author expresses itself in neologism and the extended use of familiar words, in puns and crude terms that bring a sudden sense of shock because of their unexpectedness, together with the joyous hiss of steel from rapier thrusts so delicately delivered that the wound they inflict is only appreciated a little later. The tone changes from scene to scene according to the characters present and the situation involved, but there is an overall *unité de discours* which can be recognized by its incisive wit, natural ebullience, limpid intelligence, vivid imagery and exceptional fluency, as the true voice of the author, released when he turned from *drame* to comedy, matured with his four *Mémoires* and the brilliant *Lettre modérée*, and brought to perfection when he revised the *Barbier* to its final form.

As Beaumarchais retained certain couplets and several musical interludes from the first version of the play, so he retained basically the movement and the style of an *opéra comique :* but developed to so highly sophisticated a level that a consummate technique was required of the players to achieve the necessary synchronisation of gesture, words and movement demanded by the tempo of the play. Moreover, the shape and development is such that the *guido mæstro* who mounts it must have something of the choreographer about him, if he is properly to direct the comedy which has the same element of ballet in it that the highly experienced actress Madame Dussane has noted when she played Rosine in *Le Mariage de Figaro*. There is furthermore an overall symmetry to the play that is itself a contributory factor to the swift pace. Acts I and IV, the beginning and the end, are short, while Acts II and III are long:

a brief exposition, a full development, a breathless climax. And, as in
the early scenes the audience was prepared for so much that later was
fulfilled, so the subtitle of the play, to which glancing allusion only is
made in the first half of the play, becomes the major theme of Act IV
when *La Précaution inutile* is revealed in all its useless folly.

The stage business involved in the projection of the comedy is drawn
from multiple sources—the *parades* and French farces of the period, the
conventions of *opéra comique*, and Italian comedy. There is nothing new
in the various processes by which the actors underline the wit, humour
and unfolding of the plot; the original element, as with Molière and
Marivaux, lies in the way Beaumarchais uses *lazzi* and other traditional
techniques of comedy. Nothing is extraneous in this play, and the stage
business throughout is used to expound character, link scenes, develop
the plot, assist the speed of action, even while it seems to be a purely
spontaneous outburst of energy, humour or desire to amuse the audience. Almost every page of the text offers mime, double take, exits
and entrances, disguises, concealment, and new use of well-worn
gambits, like the *lazzo* of the letter which begins Act II, Scene 12, with Almaviva disguised as a drunken cavalry officer determined to deliver his
letter to Rosine. In Scene 13 the Count rouses Bartholo's suspicions
concerning the letter, in Scene 14 substitutes another demanding that a
certain officer named Lindor (Almaviva's pseudonym) should be billeted
on Bartholo, then attempts to drop the letter so that Rosine can cover
it with her dropped handkerchief, but is forced to pick it up as Bartholo
swoops upon it, and finally hands it over and sees her put it in her pocket:
so does Bartholo, whose suspicions are not allayed by the joint attempts
of Almaviva and Rosine to deceive him. This prolonged and very
funny battle of the letter is continued in Scene 15: when Bartholo
demands to see it, Rosine pretends to faint, substitutes the letter for
another she decsribed to Bartholo while he is absent, so that he is confounded when he reads it surreptitiously while he believes her to be still
unconscious. The Act is brought to an end in Scene 16 with Rosine
alone on the stage reading her letter. Throughout, this well worn
gambit is so beautifully used, and serves to act so smoothly as a transition
from one scene to the next that it takes on a new vitality and adds a new
dimension to the comedy of those scenes.
It is also used later, and in a slightly different form, to twist the tail
of that arch-twister Bartholo; for as Rosine deceives him totally con-

cerning the letter she has in fact received from Almaviva-Lindor, so later Almaviva, this time disguised as a scholar Alonzo (Act III Scene 2), deceives him again by giving him true information and handing over a letter that Rosine had in fact written to him in the guise of Lindor; and Bartholo is completely taken in by the revelation of the exact truth made to him by one of the most interested parties in the opposite camp.

Here too, as so often elsewhere, psychological factors are added that were never present before. Bartholo is not a stupid man, except perhaps in his obsessive desire to marry his young ward; yet it is necessary for the purposes of the plot that he should from time to time be blind and deaf to matters that would normally arouse his ever ready suspicion. Beaumarchais makes clear the personalities involved. Bartholo's very obsession blinds him, and, because he is so distrustful over details, so ready to suspect the slightest and often innocent happening, he can the more easily be distracted from major causes for his constant jealousy. Almaviva's quick intelligence allows him to perceive this and to make use of it; so that in taking the grave risk of revealing a major part of the truth, and handing over the authentic letter that he had himself received from Rosine, he avoids the much graver and greater risk of Bartholo seeing through his disguise, or in any way suspecting him, in the guise of Alonzo, with amorous intentions towards Rosine. The characters of the play further the ends of the plot because they are what they are; and this also adds originality to the old traditional techniques.

No element is ignored. Figaro and others conceal themselves, over-hear counterplots, spread false information that is accepted as true, and true information that is rejected as false; there are moments of crude and hackneyed slapstick, as when Almaviva in Act II is disguised as a cavalry officer and pretends to be drunk.

Beaumarchais' inventiveness is fully demonstrated by the resource-fulness of his characters whenever they find themselves, as they so frequently do, in a tight corner. Witness Act III Scene 4, when Rosine suddenly and unexpectedly encounters and recognizes her lover, in Bartholo's presence and in his house. Her spontaneous exclamation of surprise immediately arouses Bartholo's suspicions, which are as quickly allayed by the Count suggesting to her that she has turned her ankle. The two lovers exchange a brief staccato dialogue while Bartholo goes to find a chair for her. A three-cornered conversation filled with double meanings ensues, until Bartholo, who has no ear for music, falls asleep while Rosine is having her music lesson from the pseudo Alonzo, enabling the lovers to indulge in a small orgy of hand clasping and hand kissing even as the song continues.

This musical and mimed interlude leads easily into the next scene, which offers an example of the frequent use of incongruity to heighten the comedy of the play. Almaviva and Rosine have just offered the delightful and charming picture of two young lovers wholly absorbed in each other and in the first joyous recognition of their love, symbolized in the mimed love play and the slightly *risqué* witty song sung in Rosine's clear young voice. Now, in appalling contrast to Rosine's spring song and the well-matched young pair, comes Bartholo's equally witty but utterly repugnant song, delivered in the grating cracked voice of old age and enlivened by the dance of an ancient Pantalone, whose creaking bones, atrophied muscles and spindly shanks make his intention to marry Rosine an obscenity, underlined by the supple young movements of Figaro, who, entering just then, imitates Bartholo's dance, and throws into relief all the ridiculous aspects of the old man's desires.

Mime plays a large part in the stage business involved throughout the play, as when, in this same scene (Act III, Scene 5) Almaviva tries to speak privately with Rosine, watched by 'L'œil inquiet et vigilant du tuteur' which effectively prevents the fulfilling of any such intent, even though at the same time Bartholo and Figaro are engaged in rapid dialogue.

In that act, Scenes 5-10 offer an admirable example of Beaumarchais' stage technique, in their smooth succession, and the way in which, through hilarious moments of high comedy, the immediate action is engaged while preparation is made for future manifestations, the whole expressed in brilliant dialogue and equally brilliant *jeux de scène*.

Throughout, the pace is regulated as though for a ballet, with Bartholo's absence, his return, his further absence and return, the entry of Figaro, the absence of both, the return of both, exactly synchronised with the time required for the intervening dialogue in each case.

There is also the skilful manipulation of Bazile, who seldom appears in the play, but who, whenever he does, represents a new peril to be overcome by the conspirators, or a powerful diversion when plans are going awry on either side. He is referred to for the first time in a brief scene in Act I (Scene 5) in which Bartholo, his ready suspicions once more aroused, goes out grumbling to himself 'Et Bazile qui ne vient pas!'— Bazile being revealed as the person in charge of arrangements for Bartholo's furtive marriage to Rosine. And Bazile does not come, until he makes his first appearance in Act II Scene 8 as a music teacher arriving nearly as agile and certainly as active as Figaro's, and a personality that is strong and wilful, not always pleasant but not totally unsympathetic. Rosine develops in the course of the play from the stock type of well-born young girl at the mercy of her guardian into a rebellious young woman of spirit determined to escape from the cage in which she is imprisoned; and the agent of the change is her deepening love for Almaviva. She too, gives evidence of mind, not common in the ingénues of comedy, and learns fast, as in Act II Scene 4, when she matches Bartholo in insolence and cunning; and in the same act, Scene 11, driven almost frantic by the pressures upon her, she seems to revert to her former simplicity and innocence, and with a delicate irony plays the part of the naïve young girl in such a way as to drive Bartholo to a frenzy of anger and suspicion.

The two old men, Bartholo, the guardian of Rosine, and Bazile, his friend, make a less agreable pair to complete the quartet. Bartholo, sprung from the withered loins of Pantalone, rather than from those of the Doctor Balouardo, as has been suggested, is infinitely more intelligent and cunning than either, fit match for the intelligence and cunning of Figaro. He retained the costume of his forbears, and *commedia dell'arte* marked him with the physical presentation and the mannerisms —the swooping movements, the birdlike pouncing, the agitational flutter—that belonged to the original rôle. He is an odious character; and it is wholly wrong to give him relative youth and a considerable dignity, as was done by the actor Michel de Ré in André Barsacq's production at the Théâtre de l'Atelier in 1961. Bazile is equally deplorable, and, as one would expect from Beaumarchais in a character once called Guzmann and twice Colmaro in the manuscript versions, a mean-souled man through whom Beaumarchais was able to satirize the clergy, in a way similar to the satire implied in the first two scenes of the play, when the Count was disguised as an abbé. This time Beaumarchais offers the real thing, a man whose egoism, venality and total lack of compassion or human sympathy make him a very dubious ornament of the church.

Yet these turn out to be only the superficial aspects of a quartet familiar through a hundred years or so of comedy, easily recognisable, and not profoundly original in spite of the differences from their prototypes already noted. Figaro is the catalyst here. The speed of the comedy is the speed of Figaro, verbal, mental, physical. And as, on his first entry, he

to give a lesson to Rosine. Beaumarchais having prepared Bazile's entry so much earlier in the play, now confuses his audience by leading them to expect a notary and offering them someone quite different, so that with his arrival comes a suggestion of something odd going on, which persists even when later he turns out to be a notary after all, and one deeply involved in the machinations of Bartholo.

An illuminating example of Bazile's function in the play, in the several senses of the word, is to be found in Act III Scene 11, which is also worth examining for the revelation it offers of Beaumarchais' structural skill. As the scene progresses, it can be clearly seen why it was necessary for Almaviva to gain Bartholo's confidence earlier on (Act III, Scene 2) and how absolutely he achieved this end. The comic content of the scene depends largely upon the fact that Bartholo is just as eager to keep Bazile quiet whenever the bewildered man tries to make sense of what is happening to him, as are Rosine, the Count and Figaro. But the last three have equally to prevent Bartholo as well from saying too much, and the resultant staccato doubletalk is extremely funny.

Beaumarchais also makes use, in this same scene, of the verbal repetition that is part of traditional French comedy. Examples that come easily to mind in Molière's comedies are the repetition of the words 'sans dot!' (*L'Avare*), 'Qu'allait-il faire dans cette galère?' (*Les Fourberies de Scapin*), 'Le pauvre homme!' (*Tartuffe*); or 'C'est votre léthargie' in Regnard's *Le Légataire universel*, where already there is a slightly different use, since in Molière's case the repetitions revealed character, while in Regnard's they reveal an attitude of mind. Beaumarchais makes a more sophisticated use of the same comedy technique, with much less mechanical precision about it, which serves to make it still funnier. His characters, normally on opposite sides, have only one purpose in mind in Act III Scene 11; and that is somehow to get rid of Bazile before he can say anything that will harm their different projects. Their attempts to stop him speaking suddenly change into the repeated command 'Allez vous coucher!' falsely disguised as concern for his health. All four, Bartholo, Rosine, the Count and Figaro urge him to go to bed, working up to a ridiculous climax in which the bewildered Bazile accepts their counsel and the scene ends in a plethora of 'Bonsoirs', the last repeated by Bazile himself as he goes out. There is also a certain irony in his position, that of a man more than half willing to be misled, partly because his own selfish interest is involved, partly because it may later turn out to be to his advantage to have been deceived. It offers him a way out, should one become necessary.

One of the essential parts of many French comedies was that of the confrontation of the Lady and her Lover in a scene of mock protestation and disagreement, of apparent coldness and rejection, leading to rapturous reconciliation and acceptance. In *Le Barbier* this scene of *dépit amoureux* (Act IV, Scene 7), is exceptionally short and sober, as though Beaumarchais accepted the necessity of a tradition to be found in Italian comedy, in Molière and in his own contemporaries, recognized that it was a factor in the completion of the plot and the play, yet was not disposed to linger over so well-known a gambit, and one so totally familiar to his audiences. Once more Beaumarchais evinces his masterly skill, for the scene, as fast moving as any other in the play, excludes nothing that is a proper part of this confrontation, which moves on stage in a ballet-like series of movements that swing together and apart in diagonals that sweep across the stage according to the mood and emotion of the antagonists. Yet the core of it is contained within Rosine's fiery speech of disillusion that changes swiftly to heartbreak, and the Count's reply that reveals both his triumph and his real identity. The addition of Figaro on scene, as a combined *deus ex machina* and referee of the sparring bout, adds an original and irresistibly comic effect, and serves as a link between this and the following scene in which, as Beaumarchais had described it, the young lover marries the ward 'à la barbe et dans la maison du tuteur.'

V

'La genre d'une pièce, comme celui de toute autre action dépend moins du fond des choses que des caractères qui les mettent en œuvre,' wrote Beaumarchais in the *Lettre Modérée*, which serves as preface to the published version of the play. His own characters have so ebullient and wayward a life of their own that they not only contribute to the ambiguous nature of the play and to the successful conclusion of its several intrigues, but they are at ease on each of its many levels, and touched with the same mystery of seeming to be what they are not, of expressing more than they say, which is an integral part of this comedy.

They are stock types, with characteristics inherited from the several traditions they spring from, familiar to contemporary playgoers. In Beaumarchais' hands they develop new traits, enter the modern scene with assurance; and in the course of the play become symbols of something more serious than the apparent content of the comedy would seem to warrant. They remain firmly within the framework set for them, engage themselves with the intricacies of the plot, even while they transcend both, and develop increasingly into persons in their own right, whose characters and needs promote the play, and change its nature. This duality is present in them all, and their interchanges are throughout on several different levels.

The minor rôles, the notary, the *alcade*, *alquazils*, and the like, serve to set the stage with necessary officials of a stock kind. Bartholo's two servants, La Jeunesse, and L'Eveillé, are traditional figures taken from Italian comedy and French farce, as their names indicate; for La Jeunesse is an ancient wheezing old man, a spindle-shanks all but in the grave; and L'Eveillé suffers from a perpetual yawn that reveals the drowsy stupor of what passes for his mind. They are fitting servants for Bartholo, whose avarice is implicit in his acceptance of the rejects of society to serve him, and demonstrate his desire to keep Rosine from all male contact, since neither La Jeunesse nor L'Eveillé could be supposed, even by the most jealous and suspicious guardian, to constitute any danger to her virtue. There is a noteworthy absence of female staff: a certain Marceline, who does not appear in the play or on the cast list, is referred to once or twice; but the unfortunate Rosine does not enjoy the company of a maid or confidante, or the duenna who might be expected in this case, and who was so much part of the basic comedy pattern of the time; and this lack implies much concerning the character and intentions of Bartholo. Even in these minor domestic roles there is a new approach; for Beaumarchais has stated categorically that he wished them to be played down rather than accorded the licence of the stage to these types. But it is, naturally, with the major rôles that the full impact of Beaumarchais' innovations is received.

The Count Almaviva and the beautiful Rosine are basically figures of Italian Comedy, with an aura of *opéra comique* and Racine lingering about them. Yet from the beginning they are an ardent pair full of charm and grace, speaking their reciprocal expostulation, betrayal, coldness, reconciliation and as is expected of them. Almaviva has an arrogance of manner that is absolute; he adds a quick and corrosive wit

illumines the stage, so he illumines the darkness of Bartholo and Bazile, and the love-dance of Almaviva and Rosine. He, with his gaiety of spirit and generosity of soul, his tolerance and his understanding, is the antithesis of Bartholo; with his ebullient vitality, his wit, his indestructible energy he overshadows the young lovers; and each of the four is changed because of him.

Through Figaro, Rosine finds the courage she thought she lacked, a release of spirit she did not know she possessed, an agility of mind that allows her in the end to break out of her prison. The traditional coquette in her becomes a true part of her personality, and makes her very much a young girl of the eighteenth century, at once innocent and wanton, sensitive and cruel, very feminine in her responses both to Almaviva and to Bartholo.

Through Figaro, the Count Almaviva is reduced to partnership with his valet in crime and in love, and insensibly, as the play progresses, Almaviva is diminished by this association, simply because of the effortless superiority of Figaro. A subtle part of the comedy depends upon the growing realisation that the master is less than his servant, that the servant is master himself, and *machiniste de la pièce*, as Beaumarchais described him, is manipulating the aristocratic lovers precisely as he chooses.

Through Figaro, Bazile is revealed as a half-man—half-confidant, half-musician, half-ally, half-ecclesiast—one of those creatures who live in the half light, driven by greed and self-interest to attach themselves to a stronger or wealthier entourage, envious and without any form of integrity, the betrayers of history. It was surely a Bazile who betrayed Anne Franck, or fellow Resistance workers in the last world war.

Through Figaro, Bartholo reaches his full stature, ceases to be the foolish doddering old dotard besotted with love for a girl young enough to be his grand-daughter, and is revealed as someone far more dangerous, the reactionary who dislikes the past and hates the present. In politics, in science, in literature and in love, he is an anachronism. And since he is both obstinate and obsessive—witness his attitude to Rosine—he forces his reactionary impulses to their limit of tyranny, and is revealed as the hated despot of the eighteenth century. Inevitably, he and Figaro become the antagonists of a drama contained within Beaumarchais' hilarious comedy—the conflict of the quick and the dead in human society, that is with us always. At one level they are involved in the complex unfolding of a comic plot, at another and deeper level Bartholo the reactionary, the dead man, confronts Figaro the free man, the life force; and Bartholo turns out to be a worthy opponent, with a quick intelligence, a cunning, a farsightedness to match Figaro's own. But where, with Figaro, there is joy and triumph and generosity as open and frank as the day, with Bartholo there is suspicion and jealousy and mean-souled destruction, as hidden and dark as the night.

These transformations, this struggle on another plane, bring about changes in the relations of the quartet. Rosine becomes more lovable as she becomes more spirited; so that Almaviva, himself more approachable because he is diminished, and who sets out to win Rosine by fair means or foul, finds himself, reluctantly, half-willingly, falling in love with her in a way surpassing the requirements of an amorous intrigue. Indeed though in one sense Almaviva becomes less than he was, in another sense he is more; so that, with this aura of improvement about him, he might find his natural home in the moralising *drame* that was Beaumarchais' real love in the theatre. Rosine's new spirit also affects Bartholo, who deplores the disappearance of the docile young girl he planned to make his wife without in any way consulting her over the project. The more she rebels, the more obsessed he becomes, until in the end he is discovered to be a somewhat second-rate villain after all, the victim of his own hypocrisy, jealousy and suspicion, brought down as much by the weaknesses of his own character as by the machinations of Figaro.

Only Figaro is himself throughout, just as he was the moment he first stepped upon the stage. And that first entry now can be seen to symbolize his liberty. He is a peripatetic barber, not overfond of his trade, but fond of the independence it offers him. He becomes a servant, but, as has been said, without subservience, superior to his master. He owes allegiance to no one, but will bestow it as he chooses. He outclasses his betters, is amused by his inferiors, perfectly prepared to accept what comes, and will turn it somehow to advantage. Figaro, as he made his dramatic entry on to that eighteenth-century stage, represented new ideas: that a man could have quality, whatever his origins, and perhaps more quality than those who were better born than he; that a man could be free within himself, whatever his social position. Figaro's function in the play as its core and catalyst, the man of humble beginnings who determined not only his own destiny, but that of his social betters, gave power to this new concept of liberty. His triumph over Bartholo within the framework of the comedy is also the triumph of the free man over the despot.

Beaumarchais, through his creation Figaro, gave his audiences furiously to think: and not only concerning the first breath of a liberation of the lower orders. At its most comic level, his play is non-realistic. The fortuitous encounters, coincidences and accidents, the intricacies of the plot, the overtones of conventional and stylised theatre forms, and the purposes of his several actors, make it akin to the picaresque novel so much enjoyed and appreciated by the public of his time. Indeed Beaumarchais' life is perhaps the best novel of this kind never written, for nothing in it was ever what it seemed to be: every victory turned out to be a defeat, every defeat a victory; and as fast as he was cast out or cast down, he rose again to defend himself from his enemies and his critics with whatever means came to hand. Beaumarchais in his play to some extent followed in the footsteps of Voltaire's *Candide*. He presented a stylised expression of the vicissitudes of life, moving with care and assurance in a theatrical world balanced on a tightrope between likelihood and improbability. His comedy remains one of the funniest that has ever been written, with a sober content that springs from Beaumarchais' intelligent appraisal of life as he had lived it; so that realistic and non-realistic elements blend to produce another factor in the overall ambiguity.

Beaumarchais' *Essai sur le Genre dramatique sérieux* is his testament of drama; and although both the *Barbier* and the *Mariage* are digressions from his main purpose in the theatre, they do not stem from an opposite æsthetic. Beaumarchais is perfectly sincere when he announces himself in favour of the moral role the theatre should assume, particularly since for him there was no longer any moral force or strength to be found in the Church. In his two *drames* he intended to implement his ideas, 'et offrir un intérêt plus pressant, une moralité plus directe que la tragédie héroïque et plus profonde que la comédie plaisante.' His ideas freed him from close adherence to the traditional requirements of dramatic form, and so led him to provide the pervasive feeling of liberty that is essential to true comedy, and that is to be found in its ultimate form in the *Barbier*.

Tragedy in its contemporary classic form was not able to meet the requirements of a rapidly changing society, drawing ever nearer to the cataclysm that was to tear it apart and utterly transform it at the end of the century; nor did Beaumarchais accept its premise, a belief in Fate: 'Toute croyance à la fatalité dégrade l'homme en lui ôtant la liberté hors laquelle il n'y a nulle moralité dans ses actions', he wrote. This conflict between determinism and liberty of action, which may be an illusion, but which as Voltaire said, is 'la santé de l'âme,' is the basis of

Beaumarchais' comedy, with Bartholo representing the fixed man, and Figaro the free one.

The conception of the free man, embodied in Figaro, brings with it social and political implications. These are to be found throughout the comedy, but presented as obliquely as all else, with the voices of his several characters: Almaviva, Bartholo, Bazile in differing degrees are condemned out of their own mouths; Rosine is protected by her sufferings at Bartholo's hands; and Figaro becomes the voice of the new man, with his brilliant commentary on the status quo that, like Denmark in Shakespeare's *Hamlet*, had something rotten at its core. There is here no systematized social or political criticism of the contemporary set-up, but the apparently haphazard expression of philosophical conclusions drawn from experience, of a keen sense of justice, and of a moral sense stemming from intelligent awareness and a knowledge of humanity: an unworthy and vicious man brought down, the satire of a jealous guardian, of social prejudices, of the calumnies of creatures like Bazile: a running commentary on injustice and corruption in high places.

Both Pomeau and Van Tieghem assert that the quality of the *Barbier* stems from the personality of its author. Beaumarchais, highly gifted and clearly a better man than he was ever believed to be, remains equivocal; and in this sense his play is the direct expression of himself. For there is a duality within him: on one side there is the would-be philosopher, moralist and progressive, Diderot's *homme sensible*, who wrote two *drames* before, and two others—*La Mère coupable* and *Tarare*—after his two great comedies, and who very often cast aside his moralist and intellectual pretensions. For on the other side was the entertaining cynic, the immoralist who had experienced everything, the business tycoon of dubious integrity, the brilliant wit and fast talker. All in all, a man compounded of paradox, and one well able to survive in the social, legal and political jungle.

The *Barbier* is impregnated with both sides of his complex personality; and if Figaro is a descendant in direct line of the ancient Arlecchino and Brighella of early Italian Comedy, he is also a projection of Beaumarchais who, it must be said, was himself no mean Arlequin. Any portrait of Figaro contains one of Beaumarchais, any reference to Beaumarchais' salient characteristics could be applied equally well to Figaro. Since Figaro dominates the play, fills the stage and towers over the other characters, it may well be said that the quality of the *Barbier* stems from the personality of the author; yet this is only part of the intricate truth. Beaumarchais is equally present, but unsuccessfully, in *Eugénie, Les Deux*

Amis, La Mère coupable. If the spirit of Beaumarchais pervades the *Barbier*, not all of Beaumarchais is to be found in this work. Here present is the witty author whom Voltaire could enjoy, a Voltaire too old and too well-entrenched in tragedy to feel any jealousy, too well aware of Beaumarchais' philosophical limitations to be concerned over rivalry, and eager to find a brilliant *amuseur* to carry on his own tradition of satirical comedy, albeit in another medium.

Something has survived in the play of the writer of indecent *parades*, the torch bearer of the *drame*, the man who entered zestfully into his many lawsuits and was not cast down, the self-appointed secret agent, restless vagabond, and persistent amorist; and it is the lingering essence of these facets in his personality that add to the originality of the play.

Yet, as Figaro transcends his author and, in spite of close resemblances, takes on the independent and indestructible life of the fully-created character that places him among the immortals, so the play itself, that could have come from no other hand but Beaumarchais, which is marked with his duality and his ambiguity, is nevertheless an amalgam of diverse elements, treated with great technical skill, that form a masterpiece inexplicable in simple terms. It can, like a clock, be taken to pieces to see what makes it tick; but when it is put together again it still ticks differently.

VI

Unlike Voltaire, Beaumarchais was not a dedicated artist, nor was literature more than one activity in an exceptionally full and active life. He was always hesitant as to the genre to adopt, witness the varied literary forms he used; and the apparently final versions of his work were always subject to revision. He asked for, and listened to, the advice of his friends, studied the reactions of the public, and worked closely with his actors, who played a considerable part in the deletion of certain digressions that had helped to bring about the failure of the five-act version of *Le Barbier* on stage. Yet the *Barbier* in its final form is masterly. One side of Beaumarchais suffered from intellectual yearnings. His *Essai sur le Genre dramatique sérieux* expresses his sincere preference for *drames*, which he shared in common with all contemporary thinkers, but not with the actors who came later to an appreciation of this new form, nor with the general public, who did not begin to show real interest until later in the century. The voice of the moralist speaks loud and clear in the *Essai*, in a manner that seems inconsistent, coming as it does from a writer of obscene *parades*, whose personal morality was questionable. Yet this is only a reflection of the ambivalence of the man himself. If the *Essai* bears witness to one side of his personality, the *Lettre modérée* illumines the other. It is in reality an epilogue, written when the play was already a resounding success, and Beaumarchais' private affairs were looking better than they had done for a long time. He returns here to the self-indulgent writing that had so injurious an influence upon the five-act *Barbier*. But because he is in excellent humour there are superb moments in this somewhat formless and diffuse *Lettre*, whose purpose he explained in a letter dated September 12th, 1775:

'Ma préface est uniquement destinée à montrer aux gens de lettres le cas qu'ils doivent faire de tous ces aristarques à 12 sous par feuille. En me moquant un peu de celui de Bouillon, je l'ai remis à sa vraie place, lui et sa censure, dans l'opinion publique...'

This refutation of his critics contains valuable information concerning his own attitudes to his play, and throws into high relief the other more brilliant and more cynical side of his nature.

The core of Beaumarchais' personality seems to be one of relative morality, relative integrity, and relative duplicity. He was not, nor ever tried to be, a major participant of the political scene, nor, though he would have liked to be, a great thinker, or original philosopher. He is more of an *éminence grise*, dabbling in intrigue in order to feather his own nest and because he enjoyed it for its own sake; and socially rather than politically ambitious, so that, if he kept one eye on the public, the other was always on the Court. He did not eschew the dubious, particularly if it was financially profitable; and he liked taking risks, was often carried away on the tide of his own impulse and ebullience into strange waters. He has a certain affinity with Voltaire; but he had even fewer scruples, and was less firmly held by political or philosophical allegiances. He thought and operated on a lower plane, and lacked the foresight and the vision of his great contemporary.

It is demonstrable that Beaumarchais' personality adds something to the quality of the play; but its success is broader based. The plot was already hackneyed in his own day, the conclusion obvious, and the spectator knew exactly where he stood, or thought he did. In fact he was assailed and enchanted by a shower of fireworks that lit up every nook and cranny of the comedy, illumined all its unexpected twists and turns, and, through Figaro and the speed of Figaro's thought and speech and action, whirled him off on fantastic adventures, and gave him a vicarious sense of the joy of living. Beaumarchais offered the spectator everything he could possibly ask for—something to delight both eye and ear, a promising décor, vivid imagery, beautifully controlled stage movement, light and shadow, song, music, dance. Without knowing why, maybe, he responded to the harmony of plot, gesture, mime, stage business, structure and character, constantly recognising old familiar things, constantly seeing them changed.

In this strange impure genre, the spectator is carried from a familiar into an unknown world. He looks at the puppets, the last sophisticated offshoots of a long lineage of similar puppets, and sees one among them take on new dimensions, affecting the others that cluster round him. And here comes the *frisson* of danger, of excitement beyond anything similar comedies offered. Figaro firmly and irrevocably closes the door upon the old world of servants and masters. It is a moment in the theatre similar to, but greater than, the moment when Nora slams the door behind her in Ibsen's *The Doll's House*: because afterwards nothing can ever be quite the same in a society that has witnessed these moments. Figaro, albeit unconsciously, incarnates a new force at work in the temper of the times, herald of a coming revolution and a new social order. Subconsciously, the spectator finds himself involved, putting something of his own prejudices into Figaro, and taking from him those aspects that most satisfy his particular needs. The miracle is that the titled ladies and gentlemen of the Court, who so wholeheartedly approved Beaumarchais' witty and sophisticated comedy, did not catch the distant sound of the tumbril coming closer, anymore than did Beaumarchais, or Figaro.

From whatever point of departure, discussion always returns to Figaro. It is perhaps his ability to determine events that was his greatest attraction for his contemporaries. Like Rousseau and like Voltaire in actuality, he wanders in search of peace and freedom. Man may, or may not determine his fate, but, like the Master in *Jacques le Fataliste*, a roughly contemporary production, he continues to behave as though he does. And no one more than Figaro.

Beaumarchais was a genius whose literary talent cannot altogether mask a deep flaw in his personality, and this may be, paradoxically, one of the reasons why the *Barbier* is so remarkable. For it is a masterpiece built upon a mosaic of theatrical traditions, based always upon the decadent form of those traditions, without ever becoming decadent itself. So much of it is oblique and seemingly false, but the many influences that contributed to it make a synthesis that is as delicately balanced as it is unexpected. Written at a time when a new freedom of expression was creeping into all forms of art as in social life, the comedy enjoyed a flexibility that Beaumarchais made his own.

Le Barbier has, like its author, been greatly praised and severely criticised, in its own time and throughout the years intervening. It has been lauded for its wit, brilliance, gaiety, superb construction, clarity, and verbal felicity. It has been castigated for its vulgarity, confusion, verbosity, prolixity, lack of construction, obscenity, bad taste, and dangerous social and political attitudes. Critics who prefer a pure genre, obeying strict canons of taste and conforming to classical standards, are bound to dislike *Le Barbier*; and so will those who are suspicious of verbal fluency, afraid of complexity, and unaware of subtlety. These judgments are inevitably subjective, and too often based upon insufficient knowledge of the play. One of the most astonishing comments is that of André Gide who re-read the play stretched out in a *chaise de bord* and found it had 'plus d'esprit que d'intelligence profonde. De la paillette. Manque de gravité dans le comique.' This is to remove the comedy from the stage, and so to mutilate it. It is arguable that a comedy must have intellectual depth and serious overtones to be successful. It is less arguable that Beaumarchais achieved with Figaro a creative triumph which eluded Gide; and that as soon as the play is staged it is revealed in all its glory as one of the most remarkable comedies ever written. Gide would perhaps have offered a more informed judgment had he assessed it in the theatre, where it properly belongs, and not from the depths of a deck chair. Or maybe *Le Barbier* is so impregnated with the essence of Beaumarchais that it is bound always to excite opposite opinions, from those who appreciate and those who deplore, the personality and life of its author.

The *Barbier* is unique because artists are unique, and Beaumarchais found the tone, the style, and the form that were particularly his, so that he is able to communicate with a true, if ambiguous, voice over the centuries. The insolent, glorious Figaro, with an ancestry of theatrical bits and pieces, bears witness to the creative genius of his author through his quintessential existence. Beaumarchais was an *enfant terrible*, a prodigy; and his Barber of Seville is another, mouthpiece of all mankind in his desire to be himself, to determine his own life, to achieve maximum freedom, in Beaumarchais' day as in our present time.

BIBLIOGRAPHICAL NOTE

Editions of the Text

E. J. Arnould, *La Genèse du Barbier de Séville*, Dublin University Press, and Minard, Paris, 1965, is an outstanding work of scholarship which provides us with the texts of all the manuscripts, and that of the first published edition. We have in addition precise information on the circumstances under which the play was written and produced, and new data drawn from the family archives. The only satisfactory critical edition of the text. It allows the student to draw informed conclusions.

E. J. Arnould, *Beaumarchais, Le Barbier de Séville*, Blackwell's French Texts, Basil Blackwell, Oxford, 1963, is a useful edition presenting the standard text, with the more significant variants and the salient ideas later publicised in *La Genèse du Barbier de Séville*. The introduction includes a brief account of Beaumarchais' life.

There are many other editions of the *Barbier* which are serviceable. Among these may be mentioned:

G. d'Heyli et F. de Marescot, *Théâtre complet de Beaumarchais*, Paris, 1869-1871, 4 vols. is generally considered the standard critical edition, but for the *Barbier de Séville* it is most inadequate and has been superseded by that of E. J. Arnould. A new critical edition of Beaumarchais's *Complete Works* is required.

L. Moland, *Oeuvres complètes de Beaumarchais*, Paris 1874, provides in one volume all the works of Beaumarchais known at the time.

E. Fournier, *Oeuvres complètes de Beaumarchais*, Paris, 1876, contains some new material and extracts from the *parades*.

M. Allem, *Beaumarchais, Théâtre complet, Lettres relatives à son théâtre*, Bibliothèque de la Pléiade, Paris 1934, excludes the parades.

R. d'Hermies, *Théâtre complet de Beaumarchais, présenté par Madame Dussane*, Paris, Magnard, 'Les Classiques Verts', 1952. The best edition to date of Beaumarchais' plays, although the text has not been based on the study of all existing manuscripts. There is a useful bibliography and an iconography.

M. Rat, *Théâtre de Beaumarchais*, Paris, Garnier, 1956, has often been reprinted and is generally available. *Le Barbier de Séville, Le Mariage de Figaro* and *La Mère coupable* have all been included and the introduction is particularly helpful for those who seek the links between the three plays.

L. Lejeable, *Le Barbier de Séville, accompagné d'une étude de G. Matoré sur la langue de Beaumarchais*, Paris, Brussels, Didier, London, Harrap, 1961, is chiefly valuable for its examination of Beaumarchais's vocabulary and style.

G. Bonneville, *Beaumarchais, Le Barbier de Séville*, in 'Les Petits Classiques Bordas', Paris, 1962, is a handy, inexpensive, well-illustrated, edition packed with information, suggestions, extracts from leading critics, etc. The work, however, appeared before E. J. Arnould's book and contains some errors. There are lacunae.

Bibliography

H. Cordier, *Bibliographie des œuvres de Beaumarchais*, Paris, 1883, is still a standard work of reference but should be supplemented by reference to R. d'Hermies, *Théâtre complet de Beaumarchais* listed above, to D. C. Cabeen, *A Critical Bibliography of French Literature*, vol. V, which has been brought up to date in a further volume dealing with the XVIIIth century to appear in 1968, and to *The Year's Work in Modern Language Studies*.

Biographies

P. Richard, *La Vie de Beaumarchais*, 'Les Vies privées', Paris, 1951, is the best.

M. Pollitzer, *Beaumarchais, le père de Figaro*, Paris, 1957, is aimed at the general public. The style is lively.

C. Cox, *The real Figaro. The extraordinary career of Caron de Beaumarchias*, London, Longmans, 1962, is the best English biography.

Criticism

P. Ph. Gudin de la Brennelerie, *Histoire de Beaumarchais*, ed. by M. Tourneux, Paris, 1886; and *Oeuvres complètes de P. A. Caron de Beaumarchais* by the same author, are particularly important since Gudin de la Brennellerie was a close personal friend of Beaumarchais.

L. de Loménie, *Beaumarchais et son temps*, 2 vols. Paris, 1826 and 1880, is our main source of information up to E. J. Arnould, since he had access to the Beaumarchais papers. This work was translated into English by Henry S. Edwards in 1856 (London, 4 vols.).

E. Lintilhac, *Beaumarchais et ses œuvres, d'après des documents inédits*, Paris, 1887; and *Histoire du Théâtre en France*, vol. IV, 'La Comédie au XVIIIe siècle', Paris, 1909, deal more specifically with Beaumarchais's works and analyse interestingly many of Beaumarchais' characters.

F. Gaiffe, *Le Drame en France au XVIIIe siècle*, Paris, 1910, should be consulted by students wishing to examine Beaumarchais' connection with the new genre called *drame*.

X. de Courville, *Un Apôtre de l'art du théâtre au XVIIIe siècle: Luigi Riccoboni, dit Lelio*, Paris, Droz, 1942-5, 2 vols. is equally useful on *commedia dell'arte*, coming from a scholar and a man of the theatre.

G. Attinger, *L'esprit de la Commedia dell'arte dans le théâtre français*, Neuchâtel, Ed. de la Baconnière 1950, should be consulted by students seeking to link Beaumarchais' theatre with the Commedia dell'arte.

J. Scherer, *La Dramaturgie de Beaumarchais*, Paris 1954, is a specialist study
dealing exhaustively with one important aspect of Beaumarchais' art, his
technique.

G. Von Prochwitz, *Introduction à l'étude du vocabulaire de Beaumarchais*,
Stockholm and Paris, 1956, deals with Beaumarchais' neologisms and
provides much background information, but the work is in many ways
disappointing and has been critically received.

R. Pomeau, *Beaumarchais, l'homme et l'œuvre*, Paris, 1956, is the best general
study.

J. Lough, *Paris theatre audiences in the seventeenth and eighteenth centuries*,
Oxford, 1957, provides essential background information on the world
of the theatre during the period.

J. Fabre, *Les Grands écrivains du XVIIIe siècle, Beaumarchais et le théâtre*, in
Histoire des Littératures, vol. III, Gallimard, 1958. An up-to-date general
survey.

Ph. Van Tieghem, *Beaumarchais par lui-même*, ed. du Seuil, 1960, shows us a
Beaumarchais full of sensibility and self interest being caught up in an
ambiguous philosophical position. The influences to which Beaumarchais was submitted are discussed. An excellent choice of texts adds
weight to the author's main contentions. There is a useful chronology.

J. B. Ratermanis and W. R. Irwin, *The Comic Style of Beaumarchais*, Seattle,
University of Washington Press, 1961. A substantial, but not entirely
satisfactory study dealing mainly with texts, but discussing also theories
of comedy. The analysis of Beaumarchais' comic style is insufficiently
rigorous. Concentrates on minutiæ.

E. J. Arnould, '*Le Barbier de Séville* et la Critique', in *French Studies*, XVI
(1962) deals succinctly and cogently with the reception of the play.

J. S. Spink, 'A propos des drames de Beaumarchais', *Revue de littérature
comparée*, 37, 2, 1963, deals with Beaumarchais as a writer of *drames* and
his influence in England, particularly on Colman the elder. On the
drame bourgeois see: A. R. Pugh, 'Beaumarchais, the *Drame bourgeois* and
the *pièce bien faite*', *The Modern Language Review*, vol. LXI, no. 3, July
1966, pp. 416-421.

'Th[...] read in decades
. . . Christopher Wilkins has broadened my sym-
[...]

memoir of Robert's relationship with his wife
Elizabeth and the long, sad process of her illness and
death. This is not an easy book to read – the history is
complex and the narrative is in places harrowing – but
at the same time it is charming and intriguing and I
found it impossible to put down'

BARBARA ERSKINE, *EXPRESS ON SUNDAY*

'Marvellous . . . by writing with calm, careful
precision about time, memory and love, Christopher
Wilkins has written an extraordinarily moving novel
about everything that matters'

PATRICK SKENE CATLING, *SPECTATOR*

'An intriguing meditation on time . . . Robert arrives
at a triumphant personal vision both of what constitutes love ("love is memory") and the nature of our
humanity ("memory is all we know"). In yielding to
the imperative of emotion, and acknowledging loss
and grief over and above the perfectibility of science,
the book works beautifully'

ELIZABETH BUCHAN, *THE TIMES*

Christopher Wilkins was born in Oxfordshire in 1945 and read English at King's College, Cambridge. He lives with his wife, Siân, in rural seclusion in the south of England.

THE HORIZONTAL INSTRUMENT

Christopher Wilkins

TRANSWORLD PUBLISHERS
61–63 Uxbridge Road, London W5 5SA
A division of The Random House Group Ltd

RANDOM HOUSE AUSTRALIA (PTY) LTD
20 Alfred Street, Milsons Point, NSW 2061, Australia

RANDOM HOUSE NEW ZEALAND LTD
18 Poland Road, Glenfield, Auckland, New Zealand

RANDOM HOUSE (PTY) LTD
Endulini, 5a Jubilee Road, Parktown 2193, South Africa

This paperback edition published 2000 by Anchor, a division of
Transworld Publishers

First published in Great Britain by Doubleday, 1999

10 9 8 7 6 5 4 3 2 1

A catalogue record for this book is available from the British Library

ISBN 1862 30071 2

Typeset by Hewer Text Ltd, Edinburgh

Printed by Cox & Wyman Ltd, Reading, Berks

For Siân

FIRST QUARTER

Wherever anything lives there is,

open somewhere, a register in which time is

being inscribed.

HENRI BERGSON

FIRST QUARTER

1

TIME IS MEMORY. SIMPLE AS THAT. WITHOUT MEMORY, THERE CAN
be no time. No before and after, no sooner or later, no now
and then. After all, how do we detect what we call the passage
of time except by perceiving change? But without memory, all
change would be imperceptible. We see that the leaves in the
forest are turning brown and we think, 'Autumn already. How
time flies.' But that is because we remember how the forest
looks in summer. The forest alone, denied our memories,
could not bear witness to the passage of time.

Once, when I was a child, I found a wall poster which
showed an oak tree photographed twelve times from the same
spot over the course of a year, the landscape changing with
the seasons. The poster was laid out in three vertical columns,
four pictures deep. I took a pair of scissors to it, cut out the
twelve separate pictures and rearranged them randomly into a
different pattern. Time had fled.

I organized the pictures once more into their original order
and laid them in a circle, clockwise. I had restored time, but I
had twisted it into a loop. Again I gathered them up, now
arranging them into another circle, but in an anticlockwise

direction. Time now ran backwards. I stacked them into a pile, face to face, back to back alternately, concertina fashion, so that time was trapped six times, reverberating endlessly between each pair of images. I examined each picture in turn, but time was not present within any single frame. Perhaps, as I played with the images, I was conscious on some level that time was passing, but that was time outside the photographs. The images captured by the camera were unchanging, and so not subject to time.

It did occur to me, when I was older, that the pictures, like all matter, would have been changing frenetically at the atomic level, and had I left one for any length of time in bright sunlight – in the corner of my bedroom window, say – it would have faded. But that was the thing itself, the paper, the printing ink. The photograph could bear witness to the passage of time. The tree within it could not.

2

MY WIFE, ELIZABETH, DIED SEVEN YEARS AGO, ON THE 23RD OF
April at seven minutes past three in the morning. It was a
Thursday. I know the time only from the hospital records.
They called me shortly before three to say that they thought
the end was very close and in my haste I forgot my watch. I
was twenty-five years old and it was the only human death
which had ever touched me. In England in the late twentieth
century it was possible to reach quite an advanced age
without ever seeing a dead body.

My mother had died when I was a child, before I was able to
recognize her features. The only death at which I had been
present had been that of our cat, a fastidious Russian Blue called
Pushkin who developed a nasal tumour and took to sneezing
blood and pus over our bedclothes. When the vet told us there
was nothing that could be done, Elizabeth and I agreed that the
only proper course was to have the animal put down. To spare
Pushkin the additional stress involved in driving him to the
surgery, we asked the vet to do the thing at our home. He arrived
late and flustered, smelling of peppermints and surgical spirit,
attended by a brusque, red-faced nurse.

We handed over the docile, trusting Pushkin, and while the nurse held the cat down on the kitchen table, the vet shaved a patch of fur from the back of a forepaw, produced a slender hypodermic and slid the needle under the skin. Simultaneously, Pushkin's tiny pink tongue slid out from the side of his mouth.

'Why is his tongue sticking out?' Elizabeth asked.

'He's dead,' said the vet.

It was the most startling thing I had ever seen.

'What is that stuff?' I asked him, my throat constricted by an ambush of unanticipated grief. 'Barbiturate anaesthetic. Shuts everything down instantly.' He was already packing his bag.

I looked down at Pushkin, or what had been Pushkin, and the nurse said, 'Would you like us to dispose of him for you?' And, before either Elizabeth or I had recovered sufficiently to reply, she produced a black plastic bin liner into which she dropped Pushkin's body, rolling it up and sealing it with brown adhesive tape.

What did I feel? Pain, of course. Pain from the loss of a comforting companion, a perfect creature, really. The Russian Blue is an unusual cat in some respects. It has a double coat of grey fur, unlike that of any other breed, no doubt to insulate it from the cruel winters of Arkhangel, the Russian port from which it supposedly originates, and it is the most affectionate of all cats. It loves being with people. So, yes, there was pain. But also a kind of panic, arising from the awesome and irreversible translation of the warm, companionable Pushkin

6

into . . . into what? A dead cat. In the killing of Pushkin, a line had been crossed, which could not be uncrossed.

It bothers me that I cannot know the precise instant of Elizabeth's death beyond what is written in the hospital records. Seven minutes past three. A minute seems too unwieldy a unit to mark the event. But then so does a second. And if I appear to you to calculate too coldly in this business or if I seem to deal too dispassionately with an event which should have touched me more closely than any other in my life, I hope you will bear with me for a short space because there are ways, I have found, in which a loved one may be taken from you which rob you not only of the person but of your capacity to grieve for the loss. Besides, could there ever possibly be any measurable segment of time so narrow that it cannot effortlessly be bisected by the filament that divides life from death?

3

IT WAS, I AM SURE, THIS HOROLOGICAL SPECULATION WHICH
determined me to build the watch. It was this disquiet, this
not knowing, that precipitated me into the enterprise which
came to take over my life and several times threatened to
nudge me beyond the edge of reason. An edge I fully
recognize now to be no more readily susceptible to delinea-
tion than the edge of mortality. I think at times I have been a
little mad.

Elizabeth was buried, is buried, in a small country church-
yard near the house we shared for her last two years.
Religion had never touched our lives, but when her illness
became common knowledge in the village we were hon-
oured with a visit from the local rector, who confided upon
leaving that we had the right, as dwellers in the parish, to be
buried in his churchyard. For some reason, I was greatly
taken with the prospect. So there she lies, flat on her back,
on the edge of the madly spinning globe, the night stars
streaking past her unseeing gaze at more than six hundred
miles an hour.

The earth may be considered as a large clock from which

all of our most rudimentary measurements of time derive. What we call the solar day is taken to be that interval between the two consecutive moments at which the sun appears at its highest point above the horizon, although those moments hardly ever occur at what we call midday. Sometimes the sun reaches its highest point 16 minutes and 18 seconds sooner than midday. At other times, it will get there 14 minutes and 28 seconds late. For practical needs the average length of all the solar days in a year, as measured at the Greenwich Meridian, has been calculated to produce what we know as Greenwich Mean Time, which agrees with solar time on only four days of the year, one of which happens to be Christmas day. This wanton variation is recognized on the faces of certain old English clocks, which bear what is known as an equation dial. Patek Philippe incorporated such a dial into one of their pocket watches. By a curious quirk of geography, the line of longitude which represents the Meridian runs directly through the church-yard where Elizabeth's body lies.

I am descended from a long line of watchmakers – my great-grandfather worked for the Blancpain factory in Geneva. Watchmaking is in my blood. Not only has it determined the skill of my hands, but it has also laid down, I suspect, the internal architecture of my brain. From the age of five I was taught the use of tools. My father was a great believer in protecting the young from harm not by keeping them out of harm's way but by instructing them assiduously in the nature of danger. By learning the correct protocols for the use of

9

drills, files and gravers (always keep *both* hands behind the cutting edge), my fingers were educated in the ways of sharp metal and hard materials. But the true essence of watch-making is mathematics. Put simply, a mechanical watch is a gearbox, and the ratios of those gears, and the precision with which they are constructed, determine how the watch runs. By the age of seven I was able to calculate in my head that if the balance of a watch makes 18,375 vibrations in one hour, and if the centre wheel has 80 teeth, the third wheel 70 (with a pinion of 10) and the 'scape wheel 15 (with a 'scape pinion of 8 leaves), then the fourth wheel must have 70 teeth with a pinion of 8 leaves.

It became apparent, even to a grudging taskmaster like my father, that I was something of a prodigy, and by the age of twelve I was spending every school holiday in Geneva, in the workshops of one or other of the famous watch houses. To this day, the names of those great Swiss watchmakers possess for me an incantatory potency. Piaget. Patek Philippe. Breguet. Audemars Piguet. Vacheron and Constantin. But it was not only through the handing down of his skills as a craftsman that my father laid the foundation of my future security. Long before the fashion for wearing old wristwatches reached fever pitch in the mid-eighties, he had already tucked away a handsome collection of fine pieces, any one of which would realize enough at today's auction prices to purchase a modest country estate.

Can there ever be such a thing as a perfectly accurate timepiece? In many a high street jeweller's shop window you will find displayed a mantel clock which regulates itself through radio transmissions from some remote atomic timekeeper. Self-correcting, it proclaims itself accurate to within one second over a million years. But a second is a second, even after a million years. Perfect accuracy cannot accommodate even such fine approximations.

The hoary old horologist's conceit that the only truly accurate watch is one that has stopped (the hands of a stopped watch must indicate the correct time twice during each twenty-four-hour period) is an illusion, of course, because each apparently accurate reading will in effect be a further twelve hours adrift from the previous one. Nor is the observation true, for if we pretend for the moment that there is such a thing as the 'correct' time, every watch in the world will, sooner or later, appear to show it. A watch which consistently loses five minutes in twenty-four hours will appear to tell the right time once every 144 days. A twenty-four-hour atomic clock which persists in either gaining or losing one second over the course of every million years will appear to indicate the correct time only once in 86.4 billion years. It is self-evidently futile for timekeeping purposes not to know *when* the moments of 'accuracy' coincide but, nonetheless, the observation illustrates a principle. If you have a slow-running watch, it will diverge ever further from 'correct' time with every moment that passes. As will, though in the opposite direction, a watch that runs fast.

Marine chronometers, upon which the very lives of

mariners once depended, have to be 'rated' before their readings become fully trustworthy for navigational purposes. This involves the careful notation over time of the daily rate of deviation from the Greenwich signal, or from some other regulator with a known and reliable rate of deviation of its own. The average of these readings gives the clock its 'rate', and a longer rate will tend to be more practical than a shorter one. Certainly it is safer to have a chronometer with a wide variation, provided it is consistent, than one with a smaller variation which is unreliable. It is an oft-repeated truism that no two clocks in the world, not even two atomic clocks, have the same rate.

Later, as I explored more fully the complexities of time measurement, I was to encounter the troubling discovery that many of my assumptions about horology, and indeed my instinctual understanding of the nature of time itself, were embarrassingly flawed. I came to fear that my concept of a perfectly accurate watch might be an abstraction, and I was impelled to redefine my notions of precision in less naïve terms.

It seemed to me, however, that a finely crafted mechanical movement, assiduously regulated, might periodically deviate from its own true time, first in one direction, then in the other, 'hunting', as it were, either side of the mark. But deviations such as might be caused by the effects of gravity, magnetism, variations in temperature or some infinitesimal imperfection of materials would tend to even out, producing a 'mean time' calculated not by coarse mathematics but by the accidental compounding of subtle errors, sympathetic to the inconstant flux of natural matter. It became my desire, following Elizabeth's death, to make a watch in which natural imperfections of every kind would conspire to create a flawless instrument.

4

I FIRST SAW ELIZABETH IN MY SECOND POSTGRADUATE YEAR AT Cambridge. Being a mathematical prodigy, I had taken my degree, a first in pure maths, by the age of seventeen, and had been persuaded to stay on at King's to wrestle with certain intractable paradoxes in the philosophy of mathematics. She was working in the cosmetics department of Eaden Lilley, the city's noblest attempt at a sophisticated department store, and I was helplessly captivated from the moment I set eyes on her.

She was older than I, although exactly how much older it would take me just over a year to discover. She was tiny, like a doll, with close-cropped hair the colour of scorched straw, and the jawline beneath her ears was covered in a drift of downy fuzz which the strip-lighting below the glass shop counter transmuted into an inverted golden halo. She laughed carelessly, showing snaggled white teeth, whose prominent upper canines tucked themselves away into twin dents in her lower lip. But above all it was something about her eyes which fascinated me, the darting intelligence in them, the vigilant, animal watchfulness framed in a lattice of fine wrinkles. They

14

were a myosotis shade of blue (forget-me-not, now there's an irony).

It was difficult to contrive occasions to speak with her since even the most self-confident of male students (and I was far from that) would have felt conspicuous hanging around her beauty counter debating the relative merits of Estée Lauder and Helena Rubinstein. Over a period of weeks I took to sauntering through the department at odd times during the day and if she were free I would smile at her and lean on her display case for a while, exchanging my inconsequential views on student life with hers on the retailing of cosmetics. She wore a pink tunic with a white collar, to which she had pinned a gilt plastic badge bearing the name Mrs E. Hopkins. She also wore a slender gold wedding ring. The fact that she was married in no way discouraged me, since I did not believe myself to be engaged in any serious pursuit of her. I adored her from afar. It was *amour courtois*, a dalliance, a fantasy. At least, it was until that wet Friday afternoon when she asked me out for a drink.

We agreed to meet at the Eagle, an ancient but comfortable coaching inn near the college. She was fleetingly concerned that its proximity to King's would mean exposing me to the risk of recognition and possible embarrassment should one of my fellow students chance to drop in, but I reassured her that I had no such qualms. In truth, I was secretly thrilled by the prospect of being seen with her, a beautiful, mature woman. A *married* woman, and from the town. Infinitely more glamorous than being spotted with some bouncy lacrosse Blue from Girton.

I spent the two hours and seventeen minutes before we were due to meet scouring myself from head to toe, raiding bathrooms up and down the staircase for aromatic lotions and astringents. I shaved, even though I had shaved that very morning and, to be frank, needed to shave only every two or three days at that period of my life. With mounting dismay, I rummaged through my wardrobe, whose foetid heaps of unwashed rags contrasted grotesquely in my imagination with the immaculate and, doubtless, sweet-smelling pink tunic of Mrs E. Hopkins.

I forget now what I eventually chose to wear, but I imagine the best was made of a bad job. I crossed King's Parade thirteen minutes before we were due to meet, but when I reached the Eagle, two minutes later, she was already there, without a drink, sitting in a corner at a small round table. She gave me a broad, spontaneous smile of welcome, fluttering a tiny hand above her head, in case I might somehow have failed to notice her.

'Hello,' I said, as I reached her table. 'What can I get you?'
'Into all sorts of trouble, I imagine.'

A flush of embarrassment sluiced up my neck. Standing over her I was conscious of my height, well over six feet, and of my adolescent gawkiness. She flashed her snaggled teeth again and laughed with a trilling sound as brief as the rattle of a chandelier surprised by a gust from a suddenly opened door.

'I'd love a gin and tonic,' she said evenly.

I turned away towards the bar, grateful for the chance to conceal my discomfort. I bought myself a pint of Greene King and carried the drinks back to the table.

'Well . . .' she said, as I squeezed into the corner beside her.

'Well, what?'

She raised her glass, shrugged, and said, 'Well, here we are. At last.' I stared at her, unable to form any expression on my face. She laughed again and set down her drink. 'I'm sorry,' she said eventually, 'I think maybe this was a mistake.'

'No, no,' I said, confusion shrivelling my voice to a hoarse, urgent whisper. 'It's not a mistake. How can it be a mistake? It's . . . it's lovely to see you.'

'Is it?'

'You know it is.'

'Do I?' She rested her hand briefly on mine, and grinned broadly. 'Yes, I rather think I do.'

Which was her gentle acknowledgement that I had fallen in love with her. It was true. This was more than mere infatuation, more than sexual curiosity, more than just the old familiar itch. No, this was love right enough.

Not an itch, but an ache. A deep ache that bloomed and distended through my chest, spreading up through my throat and threatening to flood my eyes with tears from the pressure of yearning to know her, and the sudden and inexplicable terror of ever having her taken from me. It was a *coup de foudre*, a bolt from the blue. It happens, believe me. If it has

17

never happened to you I feel sorry for you. Or perhaps I envy you more than you can ever know.

We sat for several minutes in silence, looking out from our corner across the bar to where a group of early evening drinkers, salesmen by the looks of them, were forging desperate merriment out of their shared frustrations and failures.

'Well, Mrs Hopkins . . .' I finally sighed.

'I think you might call me Elizabeth,' she said.

I noted then for the first time that she did not speak like a shop girl. More like a teacher or a solicitor. This pleased me, though I felt instantly ashamed of the snobbery implied by my approval.

'Well, Elizabeth . . .'

There was another long silence, after which she ventured, 'Perhaps you could tell me your name.'

'Yes, of course, I'm sorry,' I stuttered, once more wrong-footed by her taunting self-confidence. 'It's Robert. Robert Garrett.'

We sipped our drinks for a bit and I asked her, 'Why did you invite me out?'

She shrugged and looked straight into my eyes. 'I'm lonely. I don't know anyone in Cambridge.'

'You're married, though. I mean . . .'

'What *do* you mean?'

'Your name badge,' I explained lamely.

'My husband left me just over a year ago.'

At that time, I had not learned the automatic response to

such confidences. I had not yet become comfortable with the social convention of saying how sorry we are to hear something, of apologizing for things which we have not caused. What I said was, 'Were you very hurt?'

'Yes, I was.' She nodded. 'I was very hurt. Very hurt and very angry. I'm no longer angry.'

'How long were you married?'

She started to answer, caught herself, and said, 'Long enough. Long enough and happily enough to have felt utterly, utterly bereft.'

'Did he run off with someone else?'

'No. That was almost the worst part of it.' She shook her head and blinked rapidly. 'There wasn't anyone else. That would have been bad enough, I suppose. But there was nobody. It wasn't that he suddenly wanted someone else. He just didn't want *me* any more.'

'Did he say why?'

'He said that I was too nice. He said he couldn't take any more of my niceness.' She took a sip of her drink and proffered a fleeting, apologetic smile. 'Which I thought was a pretty beastly thing to say, on the whole. But why on earth are we talking about this? We should be enjoying ourselves. Tell me what you do at the university. What's your subject?'

'The philosophy of maths.'

'Golly. That sounds well over my head.'

'It's over everyone's head, I'm afraid. There's nobody in Cambridge who can really teach me any more. Nobody in England, probably.'

'How very impressive.'

'It's very troubling. I may have to go somewhere else. California, perhaps.'

'Tell me about it, your work.'

But where to start? I was always running up against this problem among my fellow students, even among students of pure maths. Bear in mind that these were the days when the name of Imre Lakatos was still virtually unknown. How could I begin to explain to people how deftly he had hurled the famous cat of Dubitability among the Foundationist pigeons? Instead, I said, 'I can tell you about the Hairy Ball Theorem.'

'Sounds faintly smutty.'

'No, it's a proper mathematical puzzle. Imagine you have a ball covered in hair and you have to smooth all the hair down. There's meant to be a topological proof that you end up either with a tuft at one end, like a coconut, or else two whorls somewhere on the surface.'

'Two what?'

'Whorls. Like you sometimes get in fingerprints.'

She studied the tips of her fingers for a moment, as though seeking some refutation of the point.

'Or there's the problem of the baby worm and the blanket,' I told her.

'There is?' she asked, widening her eyes in fraudulent wonder.

'Yes, it's really quite an entertaining idea. You have to imagine a baby worm of a certain length, whose mother wants to cover it completely with a blanket. The problem is to design a blanket with the smallest possible area which will still cover the baby worm, whatever shape it assumes.'

'Even if it's stretched out straight?'

'Oh, yes. In one dimension, the blanket must be just as long as the worm.'

She assumed a solemn expression. 'I see. Hairy balls *and* baby worms. There's clearly a lot more to this mathematics business than people think.'

I babbled on, inwardly squirming beneath her wry mockery. 'At Warwick University they're working out how to knot spheres together in the fifth dimension. Or maybe how to unknot them. There's some very strange stuff going on.'

'Gosh.'

'Yes.'

She sipped from her glass and allowed her other hand to rest once more on mine. It felt like a small bony bird settling on my skin.

'What made you first stop and talk to me in the shop?' she asked.

'I thought you were one of the most intelligent people I'd ever seen.'

She laughed softly and said, 'You can tell just by looking?'

'I believe so. You can't tell from photographs, but you can tell by the way people's faces move when they talk. Something in the eyes.'

'Could you tell from a video? Or just seeing someone on television with the sound off?'

'I'm fairly sure you can.'

'What do you do when you're not philosophizing about hairy balls? What do you do for fun?'

'Very little, I suppose.' Her question had taken me by surprise. 'I'm not really a very sociable sort of person. I don't have any friends up here.'

'Do you ever feel lonely?'

'No, not at all. I've always been comfortable with solitude and, frankly, I find most of my fellow students difficult to relate to.'

'In what way?'

'I find their thoughtlessness depressing. I can't take very much of that untiring flippancy.'

She smiled and looked down at her hands. The nails were glossy with pearly pink varnish.

'What a very serious young man you seem to be.'

'I suppose I am. But that's how I feel. Life feels to me like a pretty serious business.'

'Perhaps you need someone who doesn't take things too seriously – doesn't take *you* too seriously.'

'Maybe you're right. What did your husband do? For a living, I mean.'

'He worked for an electronics firm. That's why we came to Cambridge. For his work.'

'And you never got to know anyone here?'

She shrugged once more. She shrugged a lot, I noticed.

'We stopped going out. Together, I mean. He would leave the house in the morning before I got up and come home late at night. Sometimes he would work seventeen or eighteen hours a day. Weekends, too.'

'Do you have any children?'

'No children, no prospects. That's me.'

'Do you enjoy working in the shop?'

'I need the money.'

She finished her drink and breathed a small sigh. 'Thank you for that.'

'Would you like another?'

She shook her head and stood up. 'I have to go.'

'So soon, though?'

'I have things to do tonight.'

'Shall I see you again?'

She stared directly into my eyes once more, frowning as though struggling to decipher some difficult text. Finally she said, 'Sunday afternoon. I'll come to the college. I'll be outside the chapel at three o'clock.'

'We could go on the river. If the weather's fine, I could book one of the college punts.'

'Yes. Yes, that might be nice.'

Outside, she stood on tiptoe and let her lips brush my cheek before setting off at a brisk pace towards Great St Mary's. It had been just twenty-three minutes since I had entered the Eagle.

Dinner in hall that night was some kind of meat pie. To ease its downward passage, I queued at the Buttery bar for a pint of Audit Ale – served to me, condensation-laced, in one of those ancient heavy college beakers wrought from solid Britannia

Standard silver, whose cool, quarter-inch-thick rims could deceive you, just for a mouthful, into believing you had stumbled across a long-forgotten cache of the original ambrosial nectar. It was a great time to be in love.

5

THE NOTION THAT AN HOUR IS A FIXED AND UNCHANGING LENGTH
of time is so ingrained in us that it comes as a shock to learn
that this was not always the case. It was probably the
invention of the sandglass, some think by the monk Liutprand
of Chartres in the eighth century, which gave us our modern
notion of equally divided time. Certainly, sandglasses were
used on board English ships from around 1345, when
Thomas of Stetesham, Clerk of the King's ship *La George*,
claimed in his accounts to have purchased twelve 'glass
horloges' at Lescluse in Flanders. Such glasses would have
been used by seamen for the purposes of navigation and to
calculate the beginning and end of a watch, being referred to
in all likelihood as 'watch-glasses' – giving us the word for a
portable timepiece. (The water clock, or clepsydra, worked on
a similar principle, but sand had the great advantage of not
freezing in northerly latitudes.)

Although Christian churches were using candles grad-
uated in hours up until the fourteenth century, the formal
equalization of hours was of strictly limited use to the
scientists of mediaeval Islam, for whom the day's most

pressing and important task was the accurate determination of the hours of prayer. Hours which, because they were (and still are) calculated as fractions of daylight time, vary in length with the seasons – so that Hajji Khalifa, in his seventeenth-century encyclopaedia, dismisses both sand and water clocks as being useless for devotional purposes unless 'corrected' through traditional celestial observation.

With the adoption of independent time in the fourteenth century – that is to say, timekeeping removed from any extraterrestrial frame of reference which could be arbitrarily divided up in any way that pleased the whim of the glass blower, or soon after him the clockmaker – the sundial enjoyed a necessary renaissance. Sundials had first been employed by the Greeks in the fourth century BC, and many of those early instruments were mathematically refined, leading, it is supposed, to the growth of research at that time into conic sections. Throughout the Middle Ages, however, only a handful of scholars took any interest in sundials, and those few were more impressed by the astrolabe, which had swept across Europe from the Islamic world.

The invention of weight-driven mechanical clocks in the early fourteenth century brought with it a new role for the humble sundial, because, although the mechanical devices were self-powered, reliant on no external reference, they were not self-regulating: in order to govern the accuracy of their timekeeping, constant checks had to be made on the position of the sun. These early weight-driven clocks were provided with sundials for this purpose, and the first watches carried string gnomon sundials inside their lids.

The problem which arose, and which led to a dramatic change in the construction of sundials, was that for practical purposes mechanical clocks and watches are only comfortable coping with time divided into equal units, typically one twenty-fourth of a complete rotation of the earth, a period known as the nychthemeron. Sundials, however, certainly until the fourteenth century, had been designed to divide only each day's *period of daylight* into equal parts. But since the span of daylight varies seasonally with the declination of the sun, growing longer day by day between the winter and the summer solstices, and contracting once more over the subsequent six months, this meant that an hour in June could be roughly twice as long as an hour in December, creating within a single twenty-four-hour period what are called *unequal* hours: in summer a daylight hour would always be longer than a nocturnal hour, while in winter the reverse was true, and only at the two equinoxes would every hour be the same length.

To conform with clocks, sundials had to be redesigned to show hours of equal length, a task which required considerable mathematical ingenuity and which gave birth to a prestigious and lucrative new industry based on the science of 'dialling'. Certainly, during the fifteenth century such towns as Augsburg and Nuremberg in southern Germany profited handsomely from the trade in precision dials and other mathematical instruments.

27

The other valuable discovery from the thirteenth century which, in conjunction with these sophisticated new dials, led to the next great leap forward was the magnetic compass, which allowed sundial readings to be taken from the bearing of the sun rather than simply from its altitude. Earlier, wall-mounted dials relied upon a simple horizontal gnomon, whose shadow moved first down and then up a ladder of lines as the sun first rose then sank in the sky. Portable dials, oriented by means of a compass, could provide accurate readings from any location.

The whole of Europe went dial-crazy. Whereas prior to 1550 only four books on sundials were known outside Germany (there are no known incunabula), the rest of the sixteenth century saw the publication of thirty-nine titles, appearing in sixty-six editions – mostly, it must be admitted, in German or Italian.

Dials became highly elaborate during the course of the century, with scales and lines indicating equal hours according to the Italian way of reckoning (beginning at sunset), the Babylonian (sunrise) and the French (noon or midnight). The great diallist Giovan Battista Benedetti lists five different kinds of hour and gives seven separate methods for establishing the Meridian line. There were even dials which measured time from the rays of the moon.

In passing, if I may be indulged for a brief digression, there is a trick the French have for knowing which phase the moon has reached, whether it is waxing or waning, when confronted with an exact semicircle in the night sky. A first quarter-moon will resemble the half-disc of the lower-case letter 'p' which stands for *premier*. The last quarter-moon corresponds with 'd', as in *dernier*. Naturally, this applies in reverse in the Southern Hemisphere, although the capital 'D' can correctly stand for *Dernier* in those latitudes. The trick is mostly useless in the tropics where the lunar terminator appears pretty much horizontal in the sky.

6

THE TRADITIONAL CAMBRIDGE PUNT IS A FLAT-BOTTOMED WOODEN
craft some twenty-one feet long, with a draft of only three or
four inches. At the rear of the punt there is a platform about
four feet in length and slightly narrower in width, tapering
towards the stern and raised flush to the top of the sides. This
is where the punter stands. Or at least this is where he stands
at Cambridge. At Oxford the punter stands at the opposite
end of a craft of identical construction, where a long stretch of
the punt's floor – almost one-third of its entire length and
conveniently furnished with a ridged duckboard – provides a
walkway from which it is traditional, upon the River Isis, to
wield the pole. The Oxford man will argue forcefully for the
greater length of motive traction provided by this configuration, demonstrating that, once the pole has been dropped at
the forwardmost point of the punter's purlieu, the walk back
towards the stern of the craft maintains contact (and therefore
leverage) for the maximum length of time between the pole
and the river bed, thereby providing a greater continuity of
thrust.

The point may easily be conceded because, ultimately, it is

not a point worth making. Punting is not about efficiency, it is about elegance. It is not about force, it is about style. It is, supremely, about geometry and physics. There is a precision to controlling a punt from the Cambridge end. The pole must be encouraged to drop in a precisely vertical plane, not only relative to the fore-and-aft axis of the punt but, for absolute perfection (rarely achieved), the pole should also fall vertically relative to the transverse axis. Two separate skills must conspire to achieve the former. The first relates to the backward pressure of the water, which naturally increases with the speed of the punt. The instant you allow the end of the pole to enter the water, all kinds of impishly chaotic hydraulic pressures come into play (water being strictly non-compressible) for which you must compensate from moment to moment. The other skill lies in judging the speed of your craft – in being able to recognize the precise spot on the water's surface which is far enough ahead of your standing position that if you spear it with the pole, by the time the pole stabs the bottom, and your feet draw level with it, that sixteen-foot-long pole is vertical. The objective is to drop the pole alongside the punt in such a way that at the moment it 'bites' on the river bed and you have control, it is erect, pointing directly at the centre of the earth.

For the pole to be vertical relative to the transverse axis of the punt requires a further degree of dexterity, but it is necessary if any accuracy of steering is to be achieved. The novice may find it helpful to allow the pole to drop into the water while keeping it in contact with the metal side-strip which runs around the rear of the platform, but this trick can be dispensed with after a few hours' practice, and the pole can be slid into the water a centimetre or so from the edge of the boat, using only the punter's hand and eye to guide its path.

Once firm contact is made with the river bed, an expert punter steers his craft (and this comes as a surprise to almost everyone) mostly with his feet. As the pole bites, the hands' grasp tightens on the pole, and the feet (unshod for perfect control) grip the raised wooden surface of the platform, creating a triangular pattern of forces which allows the motion of the punt to be under continuous control until the point at which the punter judges it right to give the pole a sharp twist, freeing the inverted crescent moon of its steel tip from the river bed before launching the pole forward and upward through his loosely cradling hands to resume the whole process from the beginning.

When you get it absolutely right, the rhythm can seduce you into an almost hypnotic state where it seems as though the platform is the only still ground in the universe and your pole is repeatedly drawing the river bed and the reflected sky towards you, like pulling down an endless series of glittering window blinds.

I punted skilfully that day, with Elizabeth lying back on the bow cushions gazing up through half-closed eyes at the water-fractured sunlight rippling along the mossy undersides of the stone bridges as we slid beneath them. It was one of those afternoons in early spring when the air first shrugs off its winter chill without losing any of its winter transparency. I took us along the backs, turning round at Trinity Bridge. When we reached the Mill I hauled the punt over the metal rollers into the upper reaches which give access to the open countryside upstream.

We moored for a picnic at a bend in the river, beneath the trailing branches of willows, newly jewelled with emerald buds. We ate slim sticks of French bread, stuffing the fluffy white interior with dark rectangles of bitter chocolate broken from the bar, and we drank a bottle of the petillant rosé wine which was all the rage at that time. The meal over, we lay back on the cushions, side by side, and when I put my arm tentatively around her shoulders she burrowed closer into me, wrapping my arm more snugly about her neck and guiding my hand down through the opening of her sweater where she held it tightly pressed against one of her breasts. Never in my life had I known a happier, or a longer, moment.

7

THE CLOCKS ON SWISS RAILWAY STATIONS CAN SUSPEND TIME, and indeed do so every sixty seconds. They have plain white faces, with the five-minute divisions radially marked in bold black bars around the outer edge. The minute hand, another black bar, tapers slightly, and moves only at the end of each minute, when the sweep second hand reaches the top of the dial. The second hand is slim and red with a disc at the outer end, like a lollipop. It moves round smoothly, continuously, until it reaches its zenith at the top of the dial where it unexpectedly (and, the first time you witness it, improbably) pauses. Then, like a diver poised and focused on the lip of the high board, it topples forward, triggering the minute hand to register the passing of another sixty seconds, and simultaneously resuming its own smooth downward swoop over the dial.

Assuming the calculation to be precise (we are dealing here with the Swiss, let us remember), this must inevitably mean that the second hand is for the overwhelming majority of its life marking off the seconds a fraction faster than they are actually passing, to accumulate the small surplus necessary to fund that regular hiatus which precedes its heroic plunge from the top of the face.

8

ELIZABETH SIGHED AND TIME MOVED ON ONCE MORE.

'Whatever is to become of us?' she asked.

'We shall live happily ever after,' I told her.

'How long is ever after?'

'As long as there are two of us.'

'And we're together.'

I poled us gently back to the college, and we spent that night at her home in the Trumpington Road, in her forsaken marital bed. In the morning I learned that my father had been killed in a plane crash in northern India (when I told her, Elizabeth noted that this made us both orphans). He had gone to Kashmir to track down some of the vintage wristwatches deposited with pawnbrokers between the two world wars, either by hard-pressed colonial servants strapped for ready cash or by louche subalterns, under pressure to settle debts of honour.

There was no hope of recovering his body, so there were no funeral arrangements to be made. The Foreign and Colonial Office took care of things at the Indian end and once his death had been officially certified, my father's solicitors set in motion the process which shortly delivered his entire business interests into my hands, together with a considerable fortune. I left Cambridge without completing my research and turned my back, with surprisingly little regret, on all the arcana of mathematical philosophy. Elizabeth and I moved into my father's house in Belsize Park and the following year, when her divorce came through, we were married in Camden Register Office at half past eleven on a blustery June morning in a ceremony which lasted eleven minutes. I was twenty years old at the time. The marriage certificate revealed that she was thirty-six.

9

THE WORD 'DIAL', USED OF A CLOCK FACE, MOST PROBABLY DATES back to the *rota dialis* of the very earliest mechanical clocks. This was the wheel which, as its name implied, completed one revolution during the course of each twenty-four-hour period and was a key part of the mechanism for striking the bell to mark the passing hours. Eventually, the numbers of the hours were painted on the wheel and displayed through a window in the clock casing as a visual indicator of the time. Unlike our modern clocks, where the index or 'hand' revolves around a stationary dial, a mediaeval clock featured a moving 'dial' and a fixed hand.

Nobody knows exactly when the transition occurred between revolving dials and revolving hands, although there is some evidence that both systems coexisted in late fifteenth-century Rome. Certainly, on the outside of the fifth-century church of S. Giacomo di Rialto in Venice there is a huge blue-and-gold clock face with a single twenty-four-hour revolving hand, dating back to 1410.

Since it is the movement of the one element relative to the other which registers the passing of time, it is of no great importance which of them moves and which is stationary. Indeed, it is possible to construct a clock with gearing such as would allow both to move, and yet still indicate the correct time. It is the relationship that is critical. As a test, if we look for a moment at the face of an ordinary wall clock, then close our eyes for what we guess to be five minutes, counting off the seconds to help us, we find when we open our eyes again that the clock's minute hand is in a different position. Depending on how closely our internal mechanism for calculating time accords with that of the clock, the hand will have moved on more or less five minutes.

But determining the accuracy of our guesswork, gratifying though it may prove, is not the purpose of the experiment. The fact is that when we open our eyes we have no way of knowing in which direction the hand moved. Common sense will lead us to suppose that it went clockwise, but the new situation could just as easily be explained by the clock's winding both hands backwards eleven hours and fifty-five minutes in the opposite direction while our eyes were closed, to end up in the anticipated configuration. That it should perform such mischief is contrary to our experience, but who is to say that time itself could not behave in this way?

The seemingly innocuous question of how the idea of 'clockwise' came to represent an almost globally comprehensible pattern of movement raises a number of much more peculiar problems. There is no external physical law which dictates that the hand of a clock must always move from the vertical position downwards to the right. Mechanically, it could just as easily be made to move in the opposite direction and it is perhaps surprising that oriental cultures, whose calligraphies are written from right to left or from the bottom of the page to the top, nevertheless share the consensual notion of clockwise direction. The 'backwards' clocks which became something of a fad in the 1960s may still be found in the pages of novelty mail-order catalogues or on the walls of whimsical country pubs, and with sufficient practice it is possible to read them as readily as any other clock. The direction of movement is one which tradition, habit and preference will settle, but the thing which every one of us is most strongly disposed to believe is that the hand must move in one direction or the other. It cannot move in both. Elizabeth's death, or, more precisely, the manner of her dying, was to persuade me that this may be nothing more than superstition.

10

THE DIFFERENCE IN OUR AGES, THE REALIZATION THAT I HAD married a woman old enough to be my mother, was less troubling than may be supposed, and my initial reading of her intelligence had proved delightfully accurate. Naturally there was the occasional moment of awkwardness. She had, after all, sixteen more years of remembered experiences than I, and she was sometimes hesitant in conversation with me, catching herself embarking on a casual reference to an event which predated my birth. She was also vastly more experienced than I in sexual matters, which turned our bedroom into an enchanted kingdom of erotic discovery for me, once I had abandoned my natural male reluctance to take instruction in the finer points of carnal intimacy. That is as much as I feel that I can properly say about this aspect of our lives.

The popular music of her teenage years was known to me, but carried none of the emotional trappings with which her memories invested it. Equally, the music of my adolescence moved her not at all. Over time, we nurtured a mutual enjoyment of early chamber music, in particular that of Telemann, whose precision and simplicity appealed to my

41

sense of order while she savoured his jaunty antique elegance, both of us revelling in a feeling of nostalgia for a world equally unknown to either.

One isolated incident, though, brought home to me the magnitude of the age difference and the impossibility of my ever intimately knowing the whole of her life, of ever being able fully to fill in the details of those missing sixteen years. While we were unpacking our things in the Belsize Park house I discovered her squatting cross-legged on the bare floorboards of our new living room, surrounded by crumpled newspapers and half-emptied tea chests, poring over a thick sheaf of yellowed photocopies. I peeped at the document over her shoulder and was startled to see that the main text was in some oriental language, with tightly crammed panels of pictograms fringed with marginal notes written in blue ink in a handwriting which I recognized immediately as hers.

'Whatever's that?' I asked.

'How extraordinary,' she replied with a wistful smile. 'I didn't realize I'd kept a copy.'

'But what is it? What's the language?'

'It's eighteenth-century Manchu Chinese.'

'And you can understand it?'

'Yes . . .' She laughed. 'I still sort of can. Isn't that funny? I haven't looked at this in years.'

'What does it say?'

'It's a novel. It's the Chinese equivalent of Proust.'

'Called what?'

'Oh, it has lots of names – *The Story of the Stone*, *The Mirror of Romance* – but in the West it's mostly known as *The Dream of the Red Chamber*. It's a wonderful piece of work. You'd love it, I'm sure.'

'And are those really your notes?' I asked with a growing sense of unreality.

'Yes. I was part of a team working on a definitive translation. There are so many different versions of the text, you see – different copyists and annotators all chipping in over the centuries – that it represents quite a puzzle.'

'My God, I had no idea. Where did you learn Chinese?'

'At the School of Oriental Languages. It's not that tricky, really. All you need is a good memory and an ear for intonation.'

'Read me a bit.'

'All right. But you'll have to forgive the accent.' And she began reciting, an eerie singsong chant to which I listened in open-mouthed astonishment.

When she finished I asked her, 'What does it mean?'

She frowned for a moment, then said, 'Um . . . something along the lines of, "However much others may praise the nuptials of gold and jade, I still recall the ancient union of flower and stone, and, when my empty eyes see the beauty of pure crystal snow, I cannot help bringing to mind the lonely enchanted forest that has vanished for ever. I find that even the best of things contains some flaw. Even the kindest and most devoted of wives brings no solace to my troubled spirit." It's one of a cycle of twelve songs called "A Dream of Golden Days".'

'It's beautiful. Even in translation.'

She nodded vigorously. 'Mm, isn't it just? And it's a lot more complicated than you might imagine. There are all sorts of coded messages in it – puns and allusions. "Jade", "gold" and "snow" all refer to people in the story. And the word for "forest" – *Lin* – is the surname of Dai-yu, one of the principal female characters.'

'But why are you not still working on this? How did you end up working in a shop?'

She did one of her shrugs and shuffled the sheaf of papers together.

'Like I said, I needed the money. Our grant ran out and we couldn't find a publisher willing to take on the project.'

'And you never told me. You never once told me that you knew Chinese. I can hardly believe it.'

'A lot of men are put off by brainy women, and, besides, it's not as though it's any use to me. I'm hardly going to rush off to Beijing and become a simultaneous translator, am I now?'

'I should hope not.'

Following a brief delayed honeymoon in America, where I took the opportunity of visiting the Time Museum in Rockford, Illinois, mostly to inspect Patek Philippe's perpetual calendar watch number 861 184 with the double split-seconds hands and 'whiplash' precision regulator, our lives fell into a comfortable and reassuring routine. Three days a week I worked in my small showroom just off New Bond Street or in the workshops above. At other times the business was minded by one or other of my two apprentices – quiet, studious young men with no discernible vices or other outside interests. One was a Scot named Callum, whose hungry sunken eyes and lanky wasted frame had been handed down intact from father to son since the time of the Clearances. The other was Winston, a black lad with close-cropped hair, gold-rimmed spectacles and a neat goatee beard which gave him the air of an American business-school graduate, although he had been born and raised in Cardiff. At lunchtime they stayed at their benches, eating the sandwiches their mothers had packed for them the night before and talking in low, earnest voices not of football or girlfriends but of recoil pallets and impulse rollers. They were paragons of industry and I was always careful to praise their best work (not difficult, since it was of a very high standard) so that they should not become discouraged and be lost either to me or to the wider watchmaking community.

One of the watchmaker's most salutary skills is the mastery of that piece of machinery known as 'the turns'. This small, dead-centre lathe is such a simple device that it can be made by the watchmaker himself. It is spun by hand, using a bow – traditionally made from whalebone or cane – between whose ends a length of horsehair (originally human hair) is stretched taut. This piece of equipment, more than any other, serves to reassure the watchmaker of the value of his humanity in the face of the callous indifference of his materials. It produces such true work that I have always regarded proficiency with the turns as indispensable, even in this age of powered Swiss lathes.

My father had taught me the trick of it when I was eight years old, and at an early stage in their training I compelled both my apprentices to practise turning until they could produce three balance staffs, pivoted on one piece, similar to the submission which many years ago carried off the Worshipful Company of Turners' prize for the best specimen of steel-turning left from the graver. Through this initiation, I could rest assured that they would never lose that sense, possessed by all true craftsmen, that the quality of the final piece should embody forever within itself some echo of the maker's voice, some tremor of his hand, some molecule of his breath.

While I worked quietly away in the West End, Elizabeth threw herself with fierce enthusiasm into remodelling and redecorating our home. Starting from the basement kitchen, she worked her way up the house, transforming room after room in accordance with some instinctive notion of ideal domesticity. Her energy was stupendous. Most evenings, since she had little enthusiasm for cooking, we would eat out in one or other of the small local restaurants, and there we would talk with passion and laughter (she had taught me the trick of laughter) about every imaginable subject, unlike the stolid married couples who surrounded us, chewing their way morosely through the evening, each looking aimlessly about the room, all conversation exhausted years before.

At the end of one such meal we discussed, as we occasionally did, the difference in our ages. She asked, 'Do you think that because I'm older than you are time passes more quickly for me than it does for you?'

'Subjectively, perhaps,' I replied.

'So does time seem to have speeded up for you too? Since you were a child, I mean.'

'It seems to have done, yes.'

'By how much?'

'Difficult to say.'

'Well, think back to how long a week seemed when you were nine years old. How many of today's weeks would it take to fill a week back then? I mean, think about the week leading up to Christmas . . .'

'Three or four, maybe. Easily.'

'When you first met me,' she went on, 'I think the weeks were passing about five times as fast as they used to when I was a child. Now they've slowed down again. People say that when you get really old, time races by, like those speeded-up films of the sun streaking across the sky. Dawn to dusk in seconds.'

'I remember my grandfather telling me that time had accelerated so much for him that all he noticed was the changing seasons. He knew that time was getting on when he had to change into his winter underwear once more.'

'Why does it happen, do you think? Is it some kind of chemical change in your brain?'

'Locke believed that our train of thought moves at a constant speed, although Addison seemed to think that we could inflate our time by pumping it full of thoughts.'

'Or memories.'

'Yes, it must have something to do with memory. I mean, what else could give you your sense of how fast time passes? It's a backwards-looking thing, must be. What gives you the sense of how long a week lasts is how long you remember it lasting.'

'Which would partly depend on how much of it you noticed in the first place,' she added, 'because the less you noticed the less there would be to remember, and it would seem as though the time had been empty. Big chunks of time would become sort of . . . invisible to you. It would feel shorter than a week where you noticed lots of things going on.'

'And a child notices everything, so when you're a child each week you look back on seems filled with incident and novelty, so a week feels like a really long time.'

'Which is why,' she said, triumphantly claiming my hand across the tablecloth, 'time has slowed down again for me since you came into my life. My world is so full of new and wonderful things, I'm so much more aware of everything. When we first met I was sort of sleepwalking through life, but now I feel truly, fully conscious of every moment that passes.'

'Must be love.'

11

THE MOST IMPORTANT ITEMS IN A WATCHMAKER'S TOOL KIT ARE HIS files, of which he needs a great variety. This includes square, ridgeback, rounding-up, pillar, pottance, three-square, rat-tail and smooth. He also needs gravers (the finest are made by Vautier or Lecoutre), for cutting in the turns or on the lathe, tweezers, screwdrivers (graded in size), hammers, burnishers, nippers and pliers, various types of callipers for truing and poising, punches, vices, pegwood for cleaning out pivot holes, elderwood pith, brushes and specialized tools like mainspring winders.

His materials are steel (mild, cast, silver and high-speed), gold, silver, gemstones, brass ('red' and French), platinum, palladium, Invar or Elinvar for hairsprings, diamantine, rottenstone, tripoli, Water-of-Ayr Stone for cleaning and polishing brass, and, for the final drying-out, boxwood dust. Each material has its own dedicated use.

Diamond powder (not to be confused with diamantine), to take one example, may be used for polishing pallets on the lathe, or for grinding gemstones, diamond being many times harder even than sapphire. To prepare the rough powder for use after you have bought it (at no little expense) from your Hatton Garden wholesaler, it must first be graded by 'washing' it. For this, you need four glass jars, each containing a quantity of olive oil. Put the diamond dust in the first jar with the oil and stir it until it looks milky. After letting the coarser particles settle for about three or four minutes, pour the solution (which will contain the finer particles) into a second jar, which should be left standing for a further ten minutes. After the solution has been transferred to the third jar, the sediment remaining in the second can be used to grind stones. The third jar is then allowed to stand for half an hour, after which time the liquid contents are poured into the fourth jar. The sediment in the third jar will polish any gemstone, including a diamond. The final jar can be left for as long as necessary, with more and more of the fine particles settling at the bottom. It will be seen that the principal factors at work in this process are time and gravity.

Fresh memories are like the stirred oil in the first jar, opaque to the mind's eye. But with time, as we age, the past becomes more transparent, and only scintillae of our original experiences remain in suspension, leaving shadowy after-images in our minds. We see further, but less. Memories, like solutions of diamond dust, can be stirred, but it is the earliest memories which prove to be strongest in the end. In old age, it is often our childhood and early years which are the easiest to call to mind, perhaps because, like the first jar of diamond dust, that was where the largest particles were deposited and where stirring produces the highest density of solid matter.

12

I HAD NEVER TAKEN THE TIME OR TROUBLE TO CULTIVATE ANY friends during my stay at university and most of Elizabeth's circle seemed to belong to the period of her marriage and had either drifted away or gravitated towards her ex-husband. Many of those latter, it was irksome to discover, felt that he had been shabbily treated by her, not understanding, as we never can, the private miseries of any marriage other than our own. The only people we saw socially were Charlotte, who had shared a room with Elizabeth at boarding school, and her dreary husband, Malcolm. Charlotte was large, almost as tall as I am, and much broader, a giant slab of a woman with tumbling coils of liquorice-black hair, a jutting chin and massive feet, which she habitually forced into flamboyant red patent-leather stilettos, like a female impersonator. Malcolm was a bearded Mancunian who owned an apparently ailing sales-promotion company.

We saw them for a meal about once a month, on average. Conversation between Elizabeth and Charlotte was always easy, animated and, towards the end of the evening, even raucous. Malcolm, to be honest, I found a bit of an uphill struggle. He was one of those men who can address only one person at a time, and I was almost invariably that person. Once in a while he would turn to Charlotte, interrupting her in full flood to demand corroboration of some wearisome anecdote just vouchsafed to me (he hardly ever spoke to Elizabeth), but mostly I was his sole audience. The three of them were roughly the same age, of course, considerably older than I, which evidently imposed upon Malcolm a duty to dispense worldly advice in my direction – much of which he seemed to have picked up from the popular music of his adolescent years.

'Life is not a rehearsal,' he would tell me. 'You don't get two rides on the roundabout.' Or 'You can only play the cards the way they fall.' And even, when he was feeling particularly philosophical, 'You're a lot longer dead than you are alive.' He was a man heavily burdened with regret.

Towards the end of one such evening, having drunk an imprudent quantity of red wine in one of the local Italian restaurants, he made a rare concession to my own field of interest by abruptly pushing back the cuff of his jacket to expose a wristwatch, which he held under my nose.

'Well, what do you think?' he asked me with a smirk. 'You know all about watches, or so your good lady tells us, so what do think of this one?' It looked like a standard catalogue piece from one of the jewellery design houses, the face oblong with roman numerals on a white enamel ground, the expanding bracelet in gold and stainless steel.

53

'Very elegant,' I told him.

'Take a good look,' he urged, fumbling with the clasp so that he could hand it over to me. 'Take a close look.'

He evidently felt he was laying some kind of a trap.

'Do you think it's genuine?' he asked, his tongue nervously sweeping the corners of his mouth, but I suddenly felt too tired to play.

'It hardly matters, does it?' I told him quietly.

Sensing the tension, the women beside us fell silent.

He blinked his eyes and goggled at me in exaggerated disbelief.

'What do you mean, it hardly matters? Of course it matters. If this was genuine, you'd pay a couple of grand for it. But if it was a fake' – he paused for effect – 'which an office colleague had brought back from, say, Singapore, it would only have cost twenty quid.'

'It doesn't matter,' I told him wearily, 'because either way it's crap.'

At this he flushed carmine and snatched it out of my hand. All four of us went very quiet for a while. Eventually he said, 'How do you make that out?'

'If it's a Far Eastern fake, then it's obviously crap. But even if it is genuine, the movement inside is worth nine-teen, twenty pounds at most. That's why they give you that guarantee. Anything goes wrong with it, they throw away the old movement and put in a new one. They don't even need to employ a watchmaker – a trained monkey could do it.'

'So why would anyone pay two grand for the real thing, then?'

'Same reason they pay twenty pounds for the fake. To convince the world they've got more money than sense.'

He was breathing heavily, and it occurred to me that he might become violent, but instead of making me more cautious the prospect exhilarated me.

'So what's yours, then?' he rasped. 'What's that thing you're wearing?'

I took it off and passed it across to him. It was a 1948 Patek Philippe perpetual calendar watch in pink gold. He examined it blearily, turning it over and over in his hand. Elizabeth was smiling down at her coffee. Charlotte retrieved the watch from her husband, fearful perhaps that he might damage it, glancing at the face with polite interest as she handed it back to me.

'And what's so good about that?' sneered Malcolm.

'I just like it,' I said. 'It feels right.'

'That's it, is it? It feels right?'

'It has a very beautiful movement, wonderfully intricate. It calculates leap years.'

'Leap years, eh? Worth much, is it?'

'A fair bit, I imagine.'

'What, don't you know? How much? What would I have to pay for a watch like that? Three grand, five grand? Tell me. Don't be coy, tell me . . .'

Mindful of his belligerent state of mind and the fact that a similar watch, though in slightly worse condition, had sold at auction in Geneva the previous month for four hundred and sixty thousand Swiss francs, I said, 'Well, it's second-hand, of course, but new it would have cost something like forty-five thousand Swiss francs.' I was guessing.

'Which is how much in my money?'

'About twenty grand, at the current exchange rate.'

He leaned back in his chair, tucking his thumbs into the waistband of his trousers, a sour smile on his lips.

'You smug bastard,' he said.

Elizabeth, as a riposte, picked up a half-full bottle of San Pellegrino water and poured it over his head. It cascaded over his eyebrows, frothing and bubbling down his cheeks and through his beard. She stood up and announced, 'We really must be going. What a fun evening.'

After which it was some time before we saw them again, although in retrospect this trivial incident was to assume a greater importance in our lives than we could have anticipated.

The following morning, Elizabeth shook me awake shortly before five and whispered urgently to me in the darkness, 'My God, we were supposed to have dinner with Charlotte and Malcolm last night.'

'What are you talking about?'

'What's today? Saturday, isn't it? We said we'd see them on Friday. Last night.'

'But we did see them. You must have had a dream.'

'We saw them?' She seemed to hold her breath.

'We went to the Italian. Don't you remember? You poured a bottle of water over Malcolm's head.'

'Did I really? I can't remember a thing.'

'Too much Barbaresco.'

'Golly.'

SECOND QUARTER

Men can do nothing without the make-believe of
a beginning. Even Science, the strict measurer, is
obliged to start with a make-believe unit, and
must fix on a point in the star's unceasing
journey when his sidereal clock shall pretend
that time is at Nought.

GEORGE ELIOT

13

I BEGAN MY CONSTRUCTION OF THE WATCH ON THE FIRST anniversary of Elizabeth's death. During that initial bleak year I had visited the workshops only once, on which occasion Callum had sprung up from his workbench immediately I entered, extended his hand and said in his gentle Highland lilt, 'Sorry for your loss, Mr Garrett,' employing that easy formula passed down through generations inured to sickness and bereavement. Winston merely fixed me through his glittering lenses and nodded his awkward concurrence. I thanked them both and expressed my genuine satisfaction with how they had been running the business during my long absence. They were well out of their apprenticeships by this time, but both had chosen to remain with me. I had arranged for each of them to receive a share of the profits in addition to the generous salaries I paid them, and the business had in fact done very well.

On this second visit, I outlined to them my plan for the watch and the concomitant need for work space.

'I know this will make us a little cramped,' I told them, 'but I am sure we will manage. And since I can't possibly tell how long this piece might take to complete, it looks like you're stuck with me for the foreseeable future.'

Their instant enthusiasm was overwhelming, with all thought of their own discomfort swept aside. They seethed with questions about the project. What type of watch would it be? Would it be built on the Swiss or the English model? What kind of escapement did I have in mind? What could they bring to its construction?

Finally, to this last question, I had to reply, 'I'm sorry, but this is one I have to do all on my own. Not, as you know, that I have anything but the highest regard for the quality of your workmanship – it's not that. It's just that this is a very personal thing with me. It is something I have resolved to tackle single-handed.'

'Does it have to do with your wife?' Winston asked softly.

'It does,' I told him, 'but I can't explain it.'

'We'll keep out of your way, Mr Garrett,' said Callum, 'but we'll be here for anything you may need.'

And so it began.

The first decision I had to reach, which to someone not versed in the craft of watchmaking might seem the most arbitrary, concerned the size of the instrument. But I recognized this to be crucial. Put bluntly, a small watch cannot be expected to keep good time. The balance staff pivots in the traditional high-quality English pocket watch are only three-thousandths of an inch in diameter. Shrink the overall scale of that movement to one-quarter of its size, as many wrist-watches do, and even if you were able to machine the pivots

62

accurately to three-quarters of one-thousandth of an inch (a technical challenge, even in this day of computer-controlled lathes) the rest of the movement would be hopelessly out of proportion, particularly the escapement, whose increased inertia would contribute to a lack of consistency in the rate.

I was initially minded to copy the dimensions of Harrison's famous H-4 watch in the Greenwich Maritime Museum, which is five inches across. But this would have been a fanciful decision without any scientific justification. Bearing in mind the significant number of technical advances made since Harrison's day, I concluded that I could work confidently on a 31-lignes movement – that is, one with an overall diameter of 70mm or, roughly, two and three-quarter inches. This would, for laboratory-testing purposes, put it into the 'A' or Deck Watch category. Besides, to a watchmaker, the Harrison piece is revered largely for sentimental reasons concerning its historical context and the ingenuity of its creator. From a technical point of view it was swiftly superseded by the work of Thomas Earnshaw with his improved version of Pierre Le Roy's chronometer escapement of 1748. So remarkable, in particular, was the Earnshaw spring detent, which needed no oil, that nothing better has been found in the two hundred-odd years since its creation, and the Earnshaw escapement remains virtually unimprovable to this day.

The escapement of a watch is the mechanism which allows the power stored in the wound mainspring to be released piecemeal to maintain the vibrations of the balance. It does this by allowing the 'scape wheel to 'escape' at uniform intervals. In a sense, it snips time into a series of (ideally) equal portions, doling it out, slice by slice. It is a lurching business of stop and start or, in the case of the balance wheel, a process of repetitive rotation, first in the one direction (clockwise) and then in the other, with tiny moments of stasis between. Time inside a watch moves forward not in a steady stream, as it may appear to do for us, but in a sequence of stealthy footsteps.

14

THE DECISION TO LEAVE LONDON AND LIVE IN THE COUNTRY WAS very much Elizabeth's, and I am bound to say that it came as something of a shock to me. After less than nine months of pouring her creative energies into the house in Belsize Park, it seemed inconceivable that she should so swiftly choose to abandon it and begin again elsewhere. But her reasoning seemed to be that the pleasure lay in the doing of the work, not in its completion. Perplexed, I asked her if this meant that we would be constantly moving on like nomads each time she felt that our home was complete, but all she said was, 'Maybe not. Let's wait and see.'

Her only requirements of the new house were that it should be quiet and have an enclosed garden. After several weeks of assiduous hunting we chanced upon a handsome Queen Anne vicarage on the outskirts of a village in Sussex which, although in need of some pretty hefty restoration, had considerable charm and offered the prospect of comfortable tranquillity. It also had a squarish garden of half an acre, surrounded by high brick walls faced in knapped and dressed flint.

We sold the London house without difficulty to a City banker named Pennell Stevenson, a quietly spoken Bostonian who made no quibble over the price and who complimented Elizabeth solemnly on what he called her 'utterly inspired decorative touches' – none of which, he repeatedly assured us, did he envisage changing in the slightest degree.

Following the move to Sussex, Elizabeth seemed content enough, although she became quieter and more apparently contemplative than she had been in London, a change which I attributed to the influence of the rural environment and pace of life. The building work on the house progressed more slowly than I had been expecting, but when I asked her about it she became quite brusque and told me that she would get things organized in her own way and in her own time. This irritability was out of character and, because I could see no obvious source for it, mysterious to me.

I travelled up to town two or three days a week on the train, returning home around six. Because Elizabeth still showed no inclination to cook and there were no restaurants in the village, I would shop in London for food and prepare an evening meal for the two of us. On the days when I stayed at home with her we would eat cheese or cold meats, which I fetched from the village shop. From time to time I would propose an evening stroll to the pub, but the suggestion would for some reason agitate her, so we mostly stayed at home. It was several months before it occurred to me that she never left the house, except to walk in the garden, and that when I was away during the day she spoke to nobody except Pushkin the cat until we had him put down.

She did, however, take an interest in the garden, though in an unpredictable way. On my return from town one evening I discovered that she had engaged a firm of landscape contractors, whose initial labours had already transformed it from a place of casual natural disorder to one of almost mathematical formality. Narrow flowerbeds had been dug on all sides, turf had been laid in the centre to form a perfectly square lawn, and around this a paved walkway had been created whose edges were as straight and true as a diagram in a geometry textbook. I, as might be imagined, found its classical proportions most agreeable, although I was surprised that Elizabeth should have chosen it, given her more romantic turn of mind. The planting was equally bewildering, comprising nothing but rose bushes, all, as their identification labels testified, of the same family and variety.

'Why are all the plants in the garden the same?' I asked her after supper that night. 'Why are they all roses?'

She shrugged and looked faintly uncomfortable.

'I like roses,' she said. 'Doesn't everyone? Don't you?'

'Yes, yes. I like roses,' I told her. 'Are they scented? Will they fill the garden with wonderful perfume all summer long?'

'I've really no idea,' she said, an edge of impatience in her tone. 'They're just, you know . . . roses.'

'Fine,' I said. 'I'm really not being critical. I'm sure it will be absolutely beautiful.' But this appeared only to irritate her further.

'What are you suddenly taking an interest for, anyway? You don't give a shit about this house or the garden . . .'

'But that's not true . . .' I was dumbfounded.

'You leave it all to me. Everything. I have to cope with it all. The builders, the decorators, the sodding gardeners, it's me that has to deal with them, not you.' And she started to weep.

'Elizabeth,' I began, reaching across the table to take her hand. 'Whatever's the matter? What's wrong?'

She snatched her hand away and shrieked at me, 'What do you mean, "What's wrong?" Nothing's wrong. It's just that I can't remember flowers. I can't remember flowers. I can't remember their stupid fucking names.' I had never before heard her use coarse language.

15

IN A WATCH IT IS THE BALANCE WHICH DICTATES HOW FAST TIME IS to pass. It is the oscillations of the balance wheel which progressively permit the driving torque of the mainspring to be released through the whole escapement, ultimately to rotate the hands which 'tell us' the time. Remove the back of a traditional pocket watch while it is working and the balance will be the first thing you see in obvious motion. Usually situated slightly off-centre, towards the edge of the movement furthest from the winding crown (though there is no hard-and-fast rule about this), it will be a circular metal band, cut through in two places, often made with steel on the inside and brass on the outside, with a number of raised cylindrical screwheads protruding at intervals around the outer perimeter. It is suspended on a flat diametric crossbar through the dead centre of which passes a spindle (the balance staff) on which it 'swings' back and forth. In a high-grade movement you will see a ruby set into the balance cock above the wheel's midpoint, one of a pair of jewels into which the pivots at either end of the staff are located. On the underside of the wheel, curled up in the centre beneath the crossbar and visible from above as a pulsating dark blur, is the balance spring, also called the hairspring. Here is without question the most fragile and, so far as timekeeping is concerned, the most sensitive element of the entire movement.

Robert Hooke's invention of the spring balance some time around the year 1675 precipitated across Europe a frenzied exploration of precision mechanics which lasted over 150 years, all of it devoted to the perfecting of this tiny, oscillating spring. All kinds of metals were tried, and experiments with glass were even carried out on at least one occasion, but in the early models the material found most suitable for the purpose was hardened and tempered steel. This was not without its problems, particularly that of liability to rust, but it brought in a new standard of accuracy which, paradoxically, came to illuminate a much more persistent difficulty with the spring balance itself, namely that of temperature sensitivity.

As it warms up, the metal of the spring expands, changing both its length and its elasticity and so affecting the rate of its oscillations, in the same way that a pendulum swings more slowly as its length increases. Attempts to solve this problem gave rise firstly to an adjustment device which acted directly on the spring itself, in effect allowing the active part of the spring to be shortened, and secondly to Le Roy's invention around 1780 of the compensation balance. By fusing together two metals, steel and brass, with different expansion characteristics, the temperature errors at both ends of the scale could largely be cancelled out, particularly when fine changes could also be made to the wheel's moment of inertia by adjusting the perimeter weights and screws.

There was a series of further inventions (most notably the auxiliary compensation balance devised by Victor Kullberg for marine chronometers) designed to eliminate the frustratingly persistent problem of middle-temperature error, but the ultimate solution was to come not from refining the design of the balance wheel, so as to compensate for the instability of the hairspring, but from curing that instability at source.

The answer, which did not materialize until the early years of the twentieth century, took the form of a new alloy, called Elinvar by its inventor, the physicist Charles Édouard Guillaume, because it possessed to all intents and purposes invariable elasticity. To an existing iron–nickel alloy he firstly added tungsten and carbon, later introducing chromium to create a material whose elasticity remained almost constant in a range from freezing point to 50°C. Watchmakers could now abandon the cumbersome steel-and-brass balance and return to the uncut monometallic form (although for the most part they retained the radial timing screws around the outside of the balance rim).

For the balance rim of my watch I had intended melting down the gold from Elizabeth's wedding ring, but when the moment came to commit it to the crucible I found that I could not bear to destroy it. Its very smallness, and the unique pattern of scratches on the outer surface, scored there over the years by the uncountable actions of her vanished hand, urged me irresistibly to preserve it intact. (I have it still,

71

somewhere, in a small cylindrical box made from turned maplewood.)

Instead, I fashioned a Guillaume compensation balance from French brass, cut across, derived indirectly from Arnold's original pattern with two quadruple sets of opposing compensating screws and four platinum timing screws set at ninety degrees around the rim. Testing the truth of a balance involves the use of poising callipers, in my case of a specially adapted crossover pattern. This tool operates rather like those tricky gadgets they give you in restaurants for holding snail shells, inasmuch as when you squeeze the handles together like tongs they open and release their grip. Figure-of-eight callipers work on the reverse principle and apprentice watchmakers who have become habituated to one tool are keenly urged to avoid switching to the other; the learned reflexes wrongly applied can result in much dropped (or, worse, crushed) work.

Each of the two jaws of my callipers is jewelled with ruby endstones, and I have filed a number of serrations on the inside of one of the handles. With the balance wheel suspended on its staff between the jaws and the back end of the tool resting on the bench, the serrations are stroked gently with tweezers or a screwdriver to set the balance wheel in motion at the other end. If the wheel is perfectly poised, it will revolve at greater and greater speed. If it is out of poise – no matter how slightly – it will come to rest with the heaviest part at the bottom.

Small positional errors can be dealt with by fine adjustment to the quarter screws, drawing out one and screwing down its opposite number across the wheel until perfect poise is achieved. So sensitive is the balance wheel that it must always be handled with tweezers because even the warmth of your hand can be enough to cause the arms to bend inwards, disturbing the poise.

When the balance finally tested true, I placed it in a shallow dish of ether and blew hard on it through a tapered glass tube, evaporating the ether and thereby reducing the temperature to well below freezing point. When the balance warmed up again, I tested and adjusted it once more. I placed it in a bath of oil and heated it two or three times before allowing it to return to room temperature, poising and truing it again.

After many days of fine adjustments, the balance wheel was as true as I could make it.

16

FIVE WEEKS AFTER THE CONVERSATION ABOUT THE ROSES, I FOUND
the first of Elizabeth's lists. Written on a lined foolscap pad, it lay
on a kitchen worktop, looking at first sight like a long shopping
list, and I would have paid it scant attention but for an item near
the bottom of the page which caught my eye. It read, 'change
underwear'. I ran through the rest, which included 'clean
shoes', 'brush hair' and even 'eat breakfast'. Though baffled,
I said nothing until I found a second list tucked away in the top
of a box of paper tissues on her bedside table. This one listed
more reassuringly normal prompts such as 'call gardeners' and
'buy watering can', but also carried the instruction 'turn off gas',
which I found frankly unsettling.

When I raised the subject of these lists with her, and
confessed how they struck me as curious, she was quite
untroubled, even laughing at my concern.

'I'm such a scatterbrain these days,' she said. 'I can't seem
to keep anything in my head for more than a few moments.
I'm becoming quite like some old absent-minded professor,
you know, in those films where the lab assistant is always
saying, "You must eat, Professor . . .".'

'You forget to eat?' I asked her quietly.

'Only sometimes. I get carried away in the garden and I sort of lose track of time a bit. Only now and again.'

'How long has this been happening to you?'

" 'Happening to me"?' she snapped back. 'It isn't something that's "happening to me". I'm just a bit forgetful sometimes. It's probably lack of mental stimulation, being stuck down here in the country with nobody to talk to.'

'Perhaps we should go up to town to see a play or something,' I suggested, 'maybe have dinner somewhere really nice.'

She brightened at the prospect. 'We could call Charlotte and Malcolm. It's absolutely ages since we last saw them. Charlotte will have heaps of new gossip by now.'

I was less than anxious to renew our acquaintance with these two, being vividly mindful of the previous confrontation, but Elizabeth seemed genuinely to want to see them again, and any positive expression of will on her part was most welcome to me at this time. Nine days later the four of us were to sit down together to dine once more in the familiar Italian restaurant in Hampstead Village.

Charlotte was already at the table when we arrived, smearing pale pink lipstick across her mouth, the lips writhing and rippling against each other like a famished sea anemone. There was a half-finished drink in front of her, a negroni by the look of it, and she told us that Malcolm would be joining us later, coming on from Euston Station because he had been attending some trade fair up in Birmingham. As she prattled on Elizabeth tugged on my arm and hissed into my ear, 'Aren't you going to introduce me?'

At a loss, failing to see the joke, I said, 'Charlotte, how wonderful you look. Elizabeth has really missed you this last . . . however long it's been.'

Elizabeth looked down at Charlotte and narrowed her eyes as though trying to anticipate the mood of some unpredictable poisonous reptile. Then her face cleared and she allowed the hovering waiter to settle her into a seat, announcing, 'I'd like a drink. Charlotte, what's that you're having? No, don't tell me, I'll have a . . .' She paused, her features momentarily shadowed by panic, as the waiter bowed closer. '. . . I'll have a Ferrari. No, what is it called? A thing. A pinky thing with fizzy water, soda, yes, you know. Campari. That's it.' Triumphant.

I ordered a Peroni lager and sat down opposite her as Charlotte raised a luxuriant eyebrow and said, 'Sounds like you've had a Ferrari or two already tonight, poppet. I hope to God Malcolm isn't plastered by the time he gets here – he said to start without him. When he's been to one of these jamborees he gets drinking in the buffet car with his clients on the way back and ends up completely dismantled.'

He showed up an hour and forty-seven minutes later, swaying and sweating his way between the now overcrowded tables to join us. He seemed to have forgotten the circumstances of our last encounter because he hugged me like a favourite nephew before planting a fumbling kiss on Elizabeth's cheek, leaving a snail trace of spittle, which she

76

energetically wiped clean with her napkin and a fleeting grimace.

He slumped down in his chair, snapping his fingers for a waiter, and said, 'Sorry to be so boringly late, everyone. Trains. That sort of thing. Ah . . .' the waiter arrived, 'bring me a plate of something, can you? Pasta. Something. And a bottle of . . .' He surveyed the drink situation among the remains of our long-finished meal. 'And a bottle of Valpoliwhatsit, eh?'

Elizabeth stared at him for a moment, her eyes wide, and abruptly rose to her feet.

'I must go to the ladies',' she said.

Malcolm, chancing an ill-advised stab at chivalry, made as if to rise with her but, catching a shoe in the rung of his chair, went sprawling sideways to be caught by the waiter, who lowered him adroitly to the carpet. He struggled to his feet, flushed and rumpled from the fall, and collapsed giggling back into his seat.

'Sorry about that,' he mumbled to Charlotte, 'I had a couple of sherbets on the train with Bob Dacre.'

Charlotte pulled an ugly little pout of disapproval and made a great show of turning her attention slowly away from him towards me.

'So, how is Lizzie?' she asked. 'How is she finding life in the country?'

'To tell you the truth,' I told her, 'I believe she's a bit bored.'

'Hmm,' was all Charlotte said.

'Know who I bumped into today?' Malcolm chirped. 'You'll never guess.'

'In that case,' said Charlotte without bothering to look at him, 'there's no point in us trying.' Lowering her voice and leaning ever closer to me, she went on, 'I thought she seemed rather preoccupied tonight. Not entirely . . . with us.'

'She seems to be feeling a little . . . exasperated,' I said. 'She gets a bit snappy sometimes. With me.'

'Which is not like her, is it?'

'No, it's not. Not at all like her—'

'Bob Dacre.' Malcolm interjected. 'That's who I bumped into today.'

'Yes, you told us, Malcolm,' said Charlotte. 'You and he had a couple of sherbets on the train.'

'What an arsehole that man is. Even for a client. I'd forgotten what a complete and utter arsehole he always was.' The waiter returned with a plate of penne in garlic and chilli sauce and a bottle of red wine, which he poured for Malcolm alone, Charlotte and I both covering our glasses with our hands.

After seventeen minutes, it dawned on me that Elizabeth had not yet returned from the lavatory, which caused me an unaccountable twinge of foreboding. Possibly sensing this, Charlotte volunteered to check that 'all was well in the ladies' room'. She was back within seconds, wearing a puzzled frown.

'She's not there,' she said. 'In fact, she's not anywhere. And her coat's gone from the rack.'

I was instantly on my feet, heading for the front desk, where the girl who took the bookings and the coats (and who knew us both well) confirmed that Elizabeth had left some time before. I ran out into the street, my pulse throbbing in my throat and my mind trying to piece together an explanation for what could have happened. To be sure, Malcolm had displayed the manners of a delinquent warthog, but then he usually did, so why should Elizabeth choose this occasion to take exception and leave? I careered down the hill as far as the first side-turning, hoping to catch sight of her fleeing shape, but there was no glimpse of her. Panting, I backtracked, checking other directions. She was long gone.

When I returned to the restaurant, Malcolm was slumped forward over the abandoned table, one groping arm extended across the cloth towards Charlotte, who was leaning back in her seat, arms folded, glaring at the top of his head. She looked up at me as I arrived, rolled her eyes and asked, 'Any sign?'

I shook my head and sat down once more, frantically juggling anxiety and embarrassment. Charlotte poured me a glass of red wine and said, 'Maybe she just needed some fresh air, some oxygen to breathe. Have a drink.' She helped herself to the last of Malcolm's bottle. I drank some water and as I was glancing anxiously about, our waiter returned.

'There is somebody on the telephone for you, Mr Garrett,' he murmured. 'A gentleman.'

I took the call at the reception desk and it was only a moment before I recognized the cool New England cadences of Pennell Stevenson, the banker from Boston.

'Is that Robert Garrett?' he asked.

'Yes, it is.'

'Robert, your wife is here with me. She told me where I could reach you. I have to tell you, she seems pretty distraught.'

'Where are you? At home?'

'Yeah, we're still in your old place.'

'I'll be round right away.'

'I think immediately would be a really good idea, Robert. Elizabeth is truly not too happy right now.'

I replaced the receiver and snatched my overcoat from the rack. Back at the table, I told Charlotte about the call, and she at once said, 'Go, go, go. Don't worry about the bill, poppet – I'll use one of Malcolm's cards. Believe me, he won't feel a thing. But call me tonight, let me know what happened.'

Eight minutes later I was being ushered by a baffled Pennell Stevenson into the well-remembered living room of my old home. Elizabeth was sitting on the edge of an unfamiliar antique sofa. Her knees were clamped together, her arms were tightly curled about her, and she was rocking rhythmically back and forth, her cheeks shiny with tears in the yellow lamplight. Hearing me enter, she looked up and for a moment her face showed only panic and bewilderment until a spasm of recognition softened her expression and she jumped up to hug me.

'Thank God you're here,' she sobbed. 'Something awful has happened and I don't understand it at all. This is our house but . . . but . . . it's not our house. It's all different. My key wouldn't go in the lock and the furniture's all different, but the

80

walls and the carpets are the same. And the curtains, look at the curtains, they're right, but everything else is so very wrong and' – her voice dropped to a whisper – 'there's this man.'

I glanced back at Stevenson. 'You remember Pennell, Lizzie,' I told her. 'He bought our house. He complimented you on the way you'd done everything, your decorative touches . . .'

She drew back from me, her eyes widening. 'You sold this house?' she gasped, staring wildly around the room. 'You *sold* it? You sold our house? How could you do that?' She grew more strident, finally shrieking at me, 'You sold our house, our home? You sold our fucking home, where we live? Where will we go? Where are we going to sleep? How could you sell our home? How could you? How could you? How could you?'

'But Lizzie,' I began, 'we have a *new* house—'

'First I've heard of it,' she interrupted angrily. 'So where exactly is this new house, when it's at home?'

'It's down in Sussex. There's a big walled garden full of roses.'

She paused, open-mouthed, and subsided into calm. 'Of course there is,' she said, suddenly amused. 'Quite right. Roses. In Sussex. I got a bit confused there for a moment. Did I just say, "Where's our new house, when it's at home?"? That's rather cute, isn't it? Don't you think?'

Eighteen seconds' silence.

Stevenson, who through all this had been circling us with his back to the wall, vainly striving to keep a neutral

81

expression on his face, hunched up his shoulders, spread his palms wide at either side of his body and asked, 'Hey, can I offer you guys a drink or something?'

Elizabeth's laughter bounced around the room and she finally managed to say, 'Best not, wouldn't you say? My brain seems to be quite scrambled enough as it is. Really must learn to handle my drink better.'

I called Charlotte the following morning and passed the incident off as the unhappy consequence of Elizabeth combining alcohol with antibiotics. She hadn't drunk that much, of course. Just the one Campari and soda, hardly touched, and maybe a glass and a half of wine. So she was wrong about the drink. She was right about the brain, though.

17

IN THE YEAR OF OUR LORD 1747 IN THE SWISS TOWN OF Neuchâtel a male child was born in whom the genetic skeins had so ravelled themselves as to produce one of the few men of true genius (or so it appears to me) ever to take a contemplative evening stroll upon the face of this planet. This, it hardly needs saying to any watchmaker with a feeling for his trade, was Abram-Louis Breguet, inventor of the tourbillon. But here I am getting slightly ahead of myself because it was his first great innovation, the Breguet overcoil, which represents, to my mind, the most curious advance in the history of our craft.

No sooner had the new alloys solved the problem of temperature sensitivity in the balance spring than a fresh source of inaccuracy made itself known to the watchmaker. Once more, an apparent improvement in accuracy served only to unmask the next perpetrator of imprecision. It was swiftly recognized that even the most reliable of watches, kept in different positions, would keep different times. A watch laid flat on its back, dial facing upwards, might keep true time, but stand the same instrument on edge and its claim to accuracy would be seriously compromised.

For a time, the cause of this seemed easy enough to grasp. Surely, everyone reasoned, it must have to do with friction. Although Nicholas Facio had invented wear-resistant jewelled bearings in 1704, it had never been possible to eliminate absolutely the retardant effects of one surface rubbing upon another. So it was surmised that, when a watch is lying flat and the balance is like a child's spinning top, with the staff vertical and the wheel rotating horizontally back and forth, one pivot – the lower one – carries all the weight and the wheel will spin evenly, without undue lateral influence in any direction. In this position, described as either dial-up or dial-down, the watch is referred to as being in the 'long arcs', because the reduced friction produces a longer swing of the balance. But when the movement is pendant-up, or pendant-down, or pendant-right or -left, the pivots on either end of the balance staff, now horizontal, rest more heavily on one side of each bearing than on the other, causing an unequal distribution of friction and producing the 'short arcs'. Identifying this as the apparent cause, however, led to no solution, save the generally unrealistic one of reshaping the pivots and bearings each time the watch assumed a new position.

The practical answer sprang from the intuition of Abram-Louis Breguet in sensing that gravity itself, rather than friction, was the primary source of error and in solving the problem through the creation of a new design of balance spring which to this day bears his name. What he had come to realize was that, in a flat balance spring, the centre of gravity moves, with each swing of the wheel, alternately inwards towards the balance staff and outwards towards the regulator pins. The oscillatory frequency is affected by the earth's gravity acting more on the spring in one direction than in the other. In a similar fashion, the seas of the earth are affected most when the sun and moon both pull along a single axis, either from the same side or opposite sides of the planet.

In the Breguet overcoil the outer end of the spring is bent upwards and inwards to form a precise curve just above the main spiral. A spring of this design is said to have a uniform 'respiration' in any direction: the centre of gravity does not migrate as the spring coils and uncoils. The extraordinary thing about Breguet's invention is that he achieved it all through trial and error, through an instinctive feel for his materials and the way they behaved in nature. In fact, it was not until 1861, when Édouard Phillips published *Sur le Spiral Réglant* in Paris, that a mathematical proof of Breguet's guess-work was elaborated. But what Breguet was moving towards was what watchmakers refer to as isochronism, which literally means 'equal time'. For a watch movement to be isochronous – in time with itself – the vibrations of the balance should occur at a constant rate whether the watch is face-up, face-down or standing on its head.

In a certain rudimentary sense, metal can be said to possess a memory. If a metal poker is bent, as by that enraged visitor to Sherlock Holmes's rooms in Baker Street, it is never possible to straighten it again, as the great sleuth does, without leaving some trace of the former distortion. This is because the rod is stretched on the outside of the bend and compressed on the inside, both of which increase the hardness of the metal. Which is why, when you attempt to straighten it again (you can perform the experiment with a paper clip), it will bend most readily at a point adjacent to the previous site of damage. The metal 'remembers' what has been done to it. This is the principle behind the manipulation of balance springs.

To form a Breguet overcoil, as I had chosen to do, involves pressing the flat hairspring down onto a piece of soft wood, such as willow, with a pair of bending tweezers, determining at the first stage where the terminal curve should begin and secondly creating an 'elbow' to bring the curve back over the body of the spring towards the centre. The overcoil can further be rolled into a flawless curve by using an ivory sleeve fitted to revolve freely round a steel rod. Once bent, the spring's memory cannot be erased, only augmented by later manipulation of the overcoil, and although these subsequent tweaks and kinks serve ostensibly to quicken the short vibrations, in fact they slow down the long ones, which has the same effect on the isochronism. And if a spring has been bent too much (this happens mainly with free-sprung watches) you must always compensate by forming a new bend somewhere else; attempting to bend it back again in the same place will ruin it beyond redemption.

18

THE NEUROPSYCHOLOGIST WAS CALLED DR GONZALEZ, A SMALL, neat man whose soft voice, listing the varied eponymous afflictions to which the cerebral flesh may fall prey, wove phantasms out of the sunlit dust motes sparkling in the stale air of his consulting room. Unverricht–Lundborg syndrome, Korsakoff's psychosis, Hallervorden–Spatz disease, Alzheimer's disease, Lewy body dementia, Creutzfeld–Jakob disease. Infirmities named not for the heroes who had found their cures but merely for those inquisitive practitioners who identified and classified them, so ensuring that their own names would be feared and cursed down through the generations.

'I can be reasonably certain,' said Dr Gonzalez, 'that what we are dealing with in the case of your wife, in the case of, er . . .' – he consulted his notes – 'Elizabeth, is some type of dementia.'

The window behind him was slightly open and I could hear the intermittent rumble of traffic far below in Harley Street. They had taken Elizabeth to another part of the building, somewhere down in the basement, to carry out further tests, leaving me alone with Gonzalez for what he prefaced as 'a frank outline of the position'.

'Dementia?' I muttered. 'Do you mean that she is demented, that she is mad?'

'There are several forms of dementia,' he went on, 'and there is also a dementia syndrome, which is reversible. But this is not what we find here. What we are looking at is, I suspect, dementia of the Alzheimer type.'

'But I thought . . .' What had I thought? 'I mean, she's only thirty-eight years old. I thought dementia was a disease of the old. *Senile* dementia.'

'Not' – he leaned back in his chair and stared up at the ceiling – 'necessarily. It used to be known as senile dementia, which carried the somewhat misleading implication that it was an inevitable condition brought on by ageing, but it can occur at any age. Forty is uncommon, but not unknown. There have been cases in children as young as seven.'

His accent was that of an educated Englishman, his diction meticulous. I found myself speculating as to how a man with a name like Gonzalez could end up with such a voice – my mind drifting, postponing all consideration of the real horrors.

'When you say,' I asked him at last, 'some form of dementia—'

'Without a brain biopsy, we cannot be completely certain.'

'But . . . reasonably certain?'

'Eighty per cent certain,' he said. 'Without a biopsy, that's as close as we can get.'

'What else could it be?'

He leaned forward, setting one elbow on the desk like a man preparing for an arm-wrestling match, and counted off other diagnoses on carefully manicured fingers.

'Depression, anaemia, thyroid deficiency, a benign tumour – the scan would have picked up that last one. The condition called Lewy body dementia which I mentioned is often confused with dementia of the Alzheimer type, but it tends more to involve hallucinations – talking to imaginary friends or pets. There has been none of that, I gather?'

'No, nothing like that. What about the other things you mentioned – Korsakoff, did you say?'

'Not unless your wife is a heavy drinker.'

'What do you call "heavy"?' I asked him.

'Couple of bottles of spirits a day. Over a period of years. It's not really a true dementia, although memory loss does feature. Sufferers are usually very garrulous, can't stop talking. Often they describe extended and completely imaginary journeys they believe they have made to far-flung places. A sad and terrible affliction it may be, but it is not what Elizabeth has.'

'And the other tests – the ones you're doing now, down-stairs. Might they not—?'

'A small deception on my part, I'm afraid. I wanted to speak to you on your own so we're running a few standard tests – blood pressure, ECG, that sort of thing – to keep Elizabeth distracted for a while. It will be your decision, of course, but I strongly advise you not to tell her that she is suffering from

dementia. It will not help her to know, even if she under-
stands the implications.'

I felt uncomfortable with the way he had begun using her
name, assuming a proprietary interest as though she were an
abused child in need of protection.

'What will happen next?' I asked him. He slumped back in
his chair again, his unfocused gaze directed somewhere over
my left shoulder.

'I can't offer you much hope, I'm afraid. In fact, to be blunt'
– he looked directly into my eyes – 'I can't offer you any. Her
dementia is degenerative and unrelenting. There are one or
two drugs we might try which sometimes help with the
memory loss, but really there is no curative treatment, and
we are so far from understanding even the cause of the
condition that no cure is foreseeable. Certainly not within the
time span we are looking at here.'

'Which is?'

'With this early-onset type of condition, it could be as little
as two or three years. In older patients it can take as long as
fourteen or fifteen years to run its course, but in this case we
are talking sooner rather than later.'

So there it was. There was a sudden, scalding taste at the
back of my mouth, like copper, or blood. I felt strangely
detached, numb really, I suppose. I seemed to be moving
backwards, away from Gonzalez, who shrank to an elfin
silhouette against the pale window.

'And then she will die?' I whispered.

'Yes. I am very, very sorry.' And he startled me by slowly

shutting his eyes and shaking his head briskly from side to side as though trying to rid his skull of some disagreeable internal noise.

'Are you all right?' I found myself asking him.

'Yes, yes, forgive me.' He produced a large handkerchief from the sleeve of his jacket and dabbed at his temples. 'It's been a hell of a week, one way and another. But I'm fine, I'm fine.'

'Will Elizabeth have to go into hospital?' I asked him.

He looked down at his hands, which now rested side by side on the desk.

'Eventually, yes. But that won't be for some time, probably. Initially, you could look after her yourself, if you have the time, or you could arrange for her to have nursing care at home. She will become progressively more confused, though, and less able to do things for herself, even ordinary things like dressing and cooking. In the final stages she will be unable to speak, move, eat or drink. You will not be sure whether she can understand or even hear what you say to her. She may appear totally calm and unworried about what is happening to her, but nobody will know for certain whether that is because she has lost all conscious awareness or – and this is the spectre which haunts every one of us in this field of medicine – because she has lost only the means of expressing her distress over what is happening to her. Do you follow what I am saying? You may well want to consider finding a home for her at that point.'

'You mean a residential home, a nursing home?'

'Yes. It may prove increasingly difficult and even dangerous to cope with her in your own home, and you might well find . . .'

'I shall cope.' I was piqued.

He paused, looking sadly into my eyes once more. He knew, of course, as I could not, the dark and narrow defile into which my life would gradually become channelled in the months ahead.

'Yes, yes. I'm sure you will,' he murmured, and went on, 'There are also a number of organizations, support groups and so on – my secretary can give you the details. People find it helps.'

'How much is really known about this thing?'

'We are only just beginning to find out how little we do know. Alois Alzheimer published his paper in 1907, called "On a Distinctive Disease of the Cerebral Cortex", but the term "presenile dementia" has been around since 1868. Clearly younger people were observed to be suffering from the condition as long ago as the mid-nineteenth century. Elizabeth is obviously young – atypically young, I suppose one might say – but past the age of sixty more than one person in ten could now be affected.'

'And there really is no prospect of a cure?'

'The human brain is the most complicated object known to science and although great strides have been made with experimental surgery, imaging techniques and so forth, it remains largely a mystery. It begins to look more and more as though its very complication – its *over*complication, I would say – inevitably leads to eventual malfunction of some kind. We don't need the kind of brains with which evolution has saddled us. In competition with other species, we could survive comfortably with a tiny percentage of our thinking capacity. It is in competition with each other that our reasoning power has needed to escalate.'

I felt myself being drawn into a surreal academic debate about evolutionary theory. 'But can a species really evolve to a point where the mutations put its survival at risk?'

'Very easily. Think of a giraffe, bred taller and taller to reach higher and higher vegetation. It needs special valves in the arteries of its neck to prevent the blood rushing to its brain when it bends down to drink from a waterhole. Without them it would black out every time it drank. Even then it has to splay its legs in a cumbersome straddle, making it vulnerable to predators. Specialization brings its own problems, and for a while, perhaps, creates its own adaptive solutions.' He pinched the bridge of his nose and screwed up his eyes before resuming. 'But our own specialization has reached the point where adaptive changes cannot cope. We are like giraffes with necks thirty miles long, and there is no going back. Pretty soon, two out of five patients being treated in hospitals will be mental patients. It is as though, to use a very unscientific observation, our minds are not strong enough to handle our brains. To tell you the truth, I find it all most dispiriting, and I have yet to meet a neurologist who doesn't feel the same way.'

On the drive back to Sussex Elizabeth was heartbreakingly chirpy. We played a Monteverdi opera on the car stereo and she sang along with the soprano, not remembering the real melody lines, but making up new ones of her own and laughing helplessly when the harmonies went awry. I was apprehensive, waiting for the moment when she would ask me the results of her tests, but by the time we reached home she seemed to have forgotten about the whole trip.

Three months later, I telephoned Gonzalez to ask him about a news item in *The Times* on the causes of Alzheimer's disease – something to do with aluminium. Whoever it was that answered, a woman, told me that he was no longer with the practice and I later learned that he had died from an overdose of barbiturates a week after I had seen him.

19

IN 1996 AN EXPERIMENT WAS CARRIED OUT TO VERIFY ONE OF THE more entertaining assertions in Einstein's Special Theory of Relativity, which suggests that a clock will gain or lose time according to how fast it is travelling. Not only that, but if it is an earthly clock the direction of its divergence will depend on whether the clock moves with or against the rotation of the planet. A caesium atomic clock was placed on board a Boeing 747 airliner and flown across the Atlantic and back again, after which journey its reading was compared with that of what the designers of the experiment referred to as an 'identical' clock back in London. Upon its return, the travelling clock was found to be forty nanoseconds ahead of its sluggish, stay-at-home counterpart.

The experimenters now had two of the world's most accurate clocks in disagreement with one another. Einstein apart, which clock was right? What was the right time? It was impossible to know. Both clocks had been in constant motion before, during and after the experiment. The only difference was that during the experiment the two were moving relative to one another. From their laboratory it may have been instinctive for the experimenters to describe the result as having added forty nanoseconds to the reading on the travelling clock, but they could equally have claimed to have subtracted the same amount of time from the other one. The interpretation of events was dependent, as it always must be, on the viewpoint of the observer. From Teddington it seemed as though the airborne clock was 'going away' while the other stayed put. But were we to pretend that the aircraft remained stationary throughout, it would have seemed to those on board as though the earthbound clock had dropped away from them, moving off towards the east only to return later, more slowly, from the west, having 'lost' forty nanoseconds en route.

In any case, what is this 'second' to which we casually refer? If you heat liquid caesium-133 in an oven, leaving a tiny hole through which loose atoms can escape, you can bombard them with microwaves until they are so excited that they produce a current which can be counted in an electron multiplier. Adjusting the microwaves until the maximum current is reached creates a precise frequency of 9,192,631,770 cycles per second. That is the 'tick' of an atomic clock. But what we traditionally call a 'second' is nothing more complex than a calculated fraction of the time taken for one complete rotation of the earth. There are precisely 86,400 of them in an average day but, imprecisely, there are somewhere between thirty-one and thirty-two million of them in any given year. A second is a very rough unit indeed with which to work. Not only is there not an integral number of days in one complete earth orbit (which is why leap years were invented to balance the books), the length of those days is increasing as the earth slows. By a meticulous examination of the growth histories of coral reefs, using them as sort of palaeontological clocks, we can confidently estimate that 600 million years ago there were 425 days in a year, which means that the days were shorter or the years were longer, or both.

Since the establishment of International Atomic Time on the 1st of January, 1958, the earth and that original atomic clock have drifted thirty seconds apart in their calculations. So *now* what time is it? The planet is in continual disagreement with its best clocks, so how are we to bring them into harmony? Here pragmatism takes over and it is the clocks rather than the planet which get adjusted, because, although correcting an atomic clock may not be as simple as setting your bedside alarm, the alternative would present major difficulties.

20

FOLLOWING THAT FINAL DISASTROUS ENCOUNTER AT THE ITALIAN restaurant, Charlotte telephoned on a number of occasions. I mostly managed to intercept the calls before Elizabeth had a chance to respond, but it proved increasingly difficult to conceal the true nature of Elizabeth's illness. (Why did I feel the need for concealment? Was it some protective instinct or was it a reflection of my own persistent reluctance to admit the fatal inevitability?) But the call that came three weeks after our visit to Gonzalez put paid to all attempts to hide the truth. Returning from a mid-morning expedition to the village shop, I heard Elizabeth talking on the hall telephone. Still in her night-dress, she was speaking in a high, lilting voice. In Chinese. I stopped motionless just inside the front door until she caught my eye and her face bore such an expression of tearful confusion that I ran to her and took the receiver from her outstretched hand. Folding her to me with my free arm, I spoke into the telephone, 'Hello, can I help you?'

There was a long sigh at the other end and then the unmistakable boom of Charlotte's voice. 'What the fuck was that all about?'

'It's a long story, Charlotte,' I told her. 'Elizabeth is rather ill, I'm afraid. Let me see to her and I'll call you back.'

'I shall not leave the phone until you do.'

I managed to get Elizabeth settled into bed and she fell asleep immediately, exhausted I supposed by the exertion of struggling with her wayward memory. I tiptoed downstairs and called Charlotte. I took her through what Gonzalez had told me and she was silent for a full minute. Then I became aware of a snuffling sound at the other end and I realized that she was weeping.

'Oh, dear God,' she finally forced out. 'That is so awful. That is so fucking shitty and awful. What are you going to do? Is there anything *I* can do? Shall I come down?'

'I think it's best not to. Not right now, at any rate. It's important that I set up some kind of routine for her, apparently. Any departure from the pattern just confuses her.'

'Why was she talking Chinese to me?'

'I have no idea, Charlotte.'

'Keep in touch. Promise.'

'I promise.'

Later I was to learn that the reversion to her old field of study was not atypical. Although a time would come when by noon she would be unable to remember what she had eaten for breakfast, she would suddenly be capable of recalling long passages of oriental verse, the diamond dust of those older memories persisting more durably and accessibly than the memories of her present world.

21

THE NATURAL TIME KEPT BY THE EARTH IS KNOWN AS UNIVERSAL
Time and it was agreed in Washington, DC, at the International Meridian Conference of 1884 that each new day on the planet should dawn first on the line of the Meridian, a line defined as 'the centre of the transit instrument at the observatory in Greenwich'. The instrument referred to is the Airy Transit Circle Telescope, whose principal purpose is to establish solar time (and, thereby, GMT) by marking the precise moments when a particular star, the sun, passes through its vertical sight line.

Because of the unreliability of the earth's rotational rate, the sun rarely shows up when it ought to, at least not according to the reckoning of the atomic clock at the International Weights and Measures Office in Paris. Over recent decades, the sun has been 'slow', but there have been periods in the past, such as the years between 1838 and 1858, when the sun showed up early. Because of this wayward behaviour on the part of the planet, the atomic clock is forced to suffer the periodic indignity of being 'corrected' by human intervention. Whenever the gap becomes embarrassingly large, as large as nine-tenths of a second sometimes, a 'leap' second is added to International Atomic Time (known by its French initials as TAI), creating Coordinated Universal Time (or UTC). So it has come about that the world in general conspires to operate with a measurement of time which agrees with neither the natural motions of the planet nor the most accurate known clocks. We have, instead, a bodged compromise.

To confuse matters further, the Airy Telescope at Greenwich, being fixed on the Meridian, can also be used to mark the transit of stars other than the sun, providing us with a reading of what is called sidereal time. This accords neither with atomic time nor with solar time. Furthermore, since the observed stars are all in motion, so their positions relative to the Solar System and to each other keep changing. This apparent alteration in the positions of what were thought by the ancients to be 'fixed' stars was first noted by Edmond Halley (he of the comet) in 1718. Halley observed that three of the brightest stars were not in the positions recorded in the celestial catalogues of the Greek astronomers Hipparchus and Ptolemy. Since the rest of Halley's heavens still looked 'right' by the old catalogues, he concluded that the three stars Sirius, Procyon and Arcturus had actually changed their positions in the sky since the time of the ancient Greeks. Arcturus, in fact, seemed to have shifted by a full arc degree – twice the width of the moon as seen from the earth.

We now know that the reason these three particularly bright stars were so apparent in their motions was that they are among the nearest to us, which is partly why they are among the brightest. Just as in a given time a ship passing nearby will traverse a greater angle of our vision than a ship on the horizon travelling at the same rate of knots, so it was only the nearer stars which, until recently, had an observable 'proper motion'. But the apparent positions of all stars may be moving in a similar way. Already the artificial satellite *Hipparcos* has plotted the positions of more than 100,000 stars to within an accuracy of 0.002 arc seconds. Given that the largest observed proper motion is that of Barnard's Star, which sidles sideways across the sky at a rate of 10.3 arc seconds per year, the next satellite to take a look should be able to identify a great deal more movement.

Viewed from within our human lifespan, proper motion appears to be a slow business – there are, 1,296,000 arc seconds in a complete circle – but over millions of years the familiar constellations of today will rearrange themselves into unrecognizable patterns. So readings of sidereal time are compromised not only by the slowing of the earth but also by the gradual shifting of matter many light years distant from our world.

The accuracy of atomic clocks will, it has been predicted, continue to improve. Already a group of French scientists is claiming a tenfold improvement over the type of clock that flew the Atlantic. The inaccuracy of today's caesium clocks may be explained by the fact that the atoms being radiated within them are moving in a fast stream, and are consequently subject to a Doppler shift, which affects their frequency. If they could be slowed down or stopped altogether (perhaps using laser light) this error might be eliminated. Already they are experimenting with a caesium fountain at Teddington which may prove a thousand times more accurate. A hydrogen maser clock at the US Naval Research Laboratory in Washington has been estimated as being accurate to within one second in 1.7 million years, and there is no theoretical reason why such instruments could not be made accurate to a rate of one second in 300 million years. Eventually, with laser cooling, we could create a number of different atomic clocks, using not just caesium-133 but a range of elements (the first atomic clock used the element nitrogen and the compound ammonia). And it is predicted by at least one string theorist that those clocks will all tell slightly different times. Then what time will it be? Will we have strontium time and deuterium time as well as caesium time?

Ultimately it hardly matters, because the units of time measurement are not externally imposed. It is, and always has been, a matter of choice. If we elect to divide a terrestrial day into 86,400 bits and call each one of those a second, then that is what a second is for us. If we choose to count how long it takes 9,192,631,770 caesium atoms to be squirted through a hole and call that a second, we are equally at liberty to do so. Lengths of time are as arbitrarily and flexibly divisible as lengths of yarn.

In 1790 the French National Assembly established the length of the metre as being one ten-millionth of the distance between the equator and the north pole, as measured along a longitudinal line running through Paris. In 1983 it was redefined as the distance travelled by light in 1/299,792,458 seconds, a distance which is determined by how long we decide that a second should last. As the definition changes, so does the length. (There have been suggestions that it would be tidier to round up the figure for light speed to 300,000,000 metres per second, but this would require modifying all the standard metre measures and has so far been resisted.)

It is a ruthlessly self-referential system. We might hold a metre rule up to a prize parsnip and say, 'This parsnip is one metre long,' but we could with equal conviction state, 'This ruler is one parsnip long.' A ruler cannot be a parsnip but a parsnip can, with our connivance, be a ruler, because the quality of measurement lies in that aspect of the relationship between objects which we choose to recognize from within ourselves, from our singular point of view. A parsnip does not 'possess' length, any more than an event 'possesses' time. At its crudest, we point at one end of the parsnip and then at the other, and that which lies between the two points we call 'space'. Just as a man dying in the same bed where he slept as a child can look back to his infancy, and that which lies between then and now he calls time.

22

SEVEN WEEKS FOLLOWING THE VISIT TO HARLEY STREET, ELIZABETH wandered off in the small hours of the morning. Wearing only her night-dress, she slipped out of the front door into the lane and ambled barefoot towards the village. By chance she was intercepted by an insomniac neighbour and tactfully steered back home. She sat in the kitchen, drinking tea and glancing anxiously about.

'But where were you going?' I asked her.

'For a walk.'

'But it's twenty past two in the morning.'

'I wasn't cold, you know.'

'Well, that's something.'

She peered down at the hem of her night-dress.

'My feet are absolutely filthy,' she said. 'That bath doesn't work at all like it used to. I had a bath before we went to bed, didn't I?'

'Yes, you did.'

'Well, there's obviously something wrong with it. It must have some fault, some defect or other because just look at my feet . . .' And she laughed.

'Drink your tea,' I said.

'I'm not at all cold, you know.' She took a sip from her mug and looked around the kitchen once more. 'This is very nice,' she said. 'I wonder when they had all this done?'

'Who?' I asked, perplexed. 'All what?'

'This kitchen. Isn't it lovely?' Her eyes filled with tears. 'She always wanted a nice smart kitchen like this. She must be so pleased with it. It's made a big difference to this room, a really big difference. They must have saved up for years.' She finished her tea, crossed to the sink and rinsed the mug under the running tap. 'Time you were off.'

'What do you mean?'

'We can't have them finding us down here in the middle of the night. My father would be very upset.' She kissed me softly on the lips and said, 'I'll see you on Saturday. We can go to the pictures.'

After she had gone upstairs I sat in the darkened kitchen, unsure of quite what to do next. By believing herself to be in her parents' home while she was still living there – and while they were still both alive – Elizabeth had imagined herself back in a time long before she had met me, and yet I was evidently familiar to her. Perhaps she saw me as someone else, or had her mind reshuffled events so as to infiltrate me into an earlier period of her life? When I crept upstairs to our bedroom she was sleeping, so I inched my way in beside her. I lay awake until the sky began to lighten and I slipped into shifting dreams of falling and pursuit. In the morning she was irritable and uncommunicative, and made no mention of the night's events.

Eleven days after that, I awoke with a start in raven darkness, rain scuttling against the bedroom window and Elizabeth gone from the bed. Downstairs the front door was wide open, the hall floor spattered with wet leaves lashed in by the wind. I took the car and drove slowly towards the village on full beam, but there was no trace of her. I drove back to the house and continued on past the gates, up the lane towards the spinney, but she was not there either. Back home, I called the local police, who told me they had found a woman walking through the village in wet clothes shortly after midnight and when they had taken her to the station house she had been unable to tell them her name or where she lived. They had assumed her to be delirious and had taken her to the cottage hospital.

I found her there, sitting on a trolley, huddled in a pink cellular blanket, her bare feet swinging gently just off the floor and her hair frizzed and wild as one of the nurses finished towelling it dry. She was frowning intently at a fire extinguisher, as though trying to fathom its purpose. When I spoke her name, she looked at me with the same unchanging expression of incomprehension. I moved to hug her, but she flinched away, flapping her hands in front of her face and whimpering in panic. This rejection, which stung like a whip, was the first, yet probably the gentlest, of the myriad shafts of torment which her helpless, disintegrating mind was to inflict upon me over the coming years. Self-pity, you will call it, but when the person who means everything to you moves forever beyond the reach of pity, love or consolation you find that yourself is all that you have left to feel sorry for.

THIRD QUARTER

I confess to thee, O Lord, that I am as yet

ignorant what time is.

ST AUGUSTINE

23

BREGUET'S CONSTRUCTION IN THE YEAR 1800 OF THE *RÉGULATEUR
à Tourbillon* gave the world a device which, to all intents and
purposes, defied gravity. To free his escapement from positional error, he pivoted its balance wheel in a rotating carriage
which, driven by the watch's third wheel, performed one
complete revolution every sixty seconds. Not only did this
ensure that the balance bearings did not wear unevenly, it had
the more valuable effect of cancelling out gravitational effects
in the short arcs, no matter how the watch was held and
positioned. As far as the watch was 'aware', gravity had ceased
to exist. Breguet was granted a patent on the 10th of
November, 1801.

In this one-minute tourbillon, the averaging-out of gravitational influence happens 1,440 times in every twenty-four
hours, which provides a phenomenal degree of accuracy.
Breguet himself experimented with slower rates of revolution,
most notably with his four- and six-minute tourbillons; and in
1892 the Dane Bahne Bonniksen, who had been a teacher at
the British Horological Institute, patented his Karrusels. These
operated on the same principle, although rotating only once

in 52.5 or 34 minutes; the only identifiable advantage of these modifications was their potential cheapness of manufacture.

Without doubt, the finest timepiece ever made incorporating a tourbillon was Patek Philippe's pocket watch No. 198 411, whose construction was begun on the 10th of October, 1930, and which was sold on the 19th of March, 1952, to the Henri Stern Watch Agency in New York. In addition to the tourbillon, made by Hector Golay, it featured a Breguet overcoil (originally with index regulation but modified to free-sprung for competition purposes) and a Guillaume compensation balance.

In February 1958 it was bought back by Patek Philippe and was later entered in the Geneva Observatory chronometrical competition of 1962, where it established a record in its class that is still unbroken – although it is worth noting that the record was open to challenge for only five years, mechanical watches being no longer admitted to the tests after 1967, when the miniaturization of electronic components had made possible the quartz wristwatch. The assumption was made that quartz watches would thereafter outperform traditional mechanical movements, but this remains an assumption whose validity will increasingly depend on our view of time and what it is exactly that we are attempting to measure.

24

THE ONLY WAY TO ENSURE ELIZABETH'S SAFETY IN THE FACE OF HER nocturnal excursions was to imprison her at night. I had new locks fitted to all the doors and windows, and kept the keys on a chain around my neck. Every other night for the first week or so she would creep from the bedroom and I would hear her rattling the front-door latch, gingerly to begin with and then with mounting fury (or was it alarm?) until she began hammering on the panels and shrieking to be let out. When I went down to her, sometimes she would become instantly calm and allow me to lead her back upstairs to bed. At other times she would turn on me, hissing and gibbering and pounding on my chest and shoulders with her fists. Eventually, I lit upon the idea of leaving her sandals by the open door to the garden, and this seemed to satisfy her need to walk. I could watch her from the bedroom window on moonlit nights as she paced tirelessly between the roses, always in the same direction, anticlockwise, and taking always the same number of paces on each side of the square, as though she were counting them in her head. Some nights she would walk for three or four hours without resting, and when she came in she would let me bathe her swollen feet in cool water and carry her back upstairs, where she would drift off to sleep, hugging her tattered sandals to her breast.

As we become aware that our memory may be failing there are strategies we can adopt, at least in the early stages; Elizabeth had recognized this with her lists. We can create patterns, repetitive actions that give a shape and a predictability to the world, a continuity to our experiences. But take away our consciousness, interrupt the pattern by even so little as an hour's sleep, and that artificial continuity is lost. Have you never awoken on the first morning of a foreign holiday, momentarily confused by the strangeness of the hotel room, the unrecognizable furniture, the window in the wrong place? And have you not then felt a similar shock of alienation upon waking for the first time back home again, after the holiday is over, in your own familiar bedroom? The moment passes, the uneasiness abates, the mind swiftly reimposes a sense of reality.

But what if it did not? Imagine the terror. What if everything remained strange and refused to be reassembled into a recognizable universe? What if there were maybe only a small number of things that you could remember ever having seen before? Perhaps just the one thing. Perhaps you can recognize only a pair of shoes and everything else is different. Think how you would cling to those shoes, your only friends from yesterday's world.

During the hours of daylight, Elizabeth seemed less agitated. She had taken up tapestry work, and this would occupy

114

her for hours at a stretch. I believe she found a kind of sanctuary in its predictability, in the repetition, the way it grew slowly, making no sudden moves, doing nothing that would jar her into confrontation with the changing reality around her. She made no attempt to create figurative images but simply worked across from left to right, line by line, beginning at the top and using whatever coloured wools came to hand. The resulting abstract patterns were of no apparent interest to her and, upon finishing one piece, she would immediately begin another, using the wool that still remained in her needle.

The daytime, though, was not without its own frustrations. During her severest bouts of memory loss, she would ask me the same question over and over again.

'What are we having for lunch today?'

'Salmon. Would you like that?'

'How will you do it?'

'In foil. In the oven.'

'Will there be vegetables?'

'New potatoes.'

'That's nice.'

After ten minutes of smiling contemplation, she would frown and ask, 'What are we having for lunch today?'

'Salmon. You like that, don't you?'

'How will you cook it?'

'I shall bake it in the oven. In foil.'

'Will there be any vegetables?'

'Potatoes. New potatoes, with butter and mint.'

'Sounds nice.'

Sometimes these sessions would go on for almost an hour, and, no matter how patiently I tried to answer her questions, an anger and a frustration would begin to build in me, and even a suspicion that there was a degree of mischief – or, worse, malice – in her smiling interrogation. Just as a child learns to manipulate its parents into a state of exasperation through repeated questioning, so it was hard to believe she was not somehow putting on an act.

'What are we having for lunch today?'

'Salmon.'

'How will you cook it?'

'In the oven'

'Will there be vegetables?'

'Potatoes!' I would shout at her. 'For Christ's sake. New potatoes. How many more times do you want me to tell you?' And she would look hurt and I would feel drenched in guilt as her lip would start to quiver and tears would fill her eyes and I would put my arms around her, hugging her to my chest until she had calmed down enough to ask:

'What are we having for lunch today?'

Then I would have to leave the room. Sometimes I would have to leave the house and stride up the lane to the spinney, where I would stand howling and roaring my frustration into the uncomprehending silver birches. Leaving her alone for even a short time increased her attachment to me, so that she began following me around from room to room as soon as I returned, and showed signs of agitation if she lost sight of me for more than a few moments. It became apparent that I would no longer be able to go up to London, leaving her on her own, which is how I came to entrust the business to my two apprentices.

Even shopping was a problem. When I left her for twenty minutes to go into the village, locking her in – though fearful of her setting fire to the house and becoming trapped – I would return to find her in a state of fluttering panic, accusing me tearfully of having been away for hours. This was when she first began to slip the leash of linear time. Her internal sense of duration had been eroded to the point where the evidence of clocks made little sense and only fuelled her suspicions about the unreliability of external signs.

To calm her during my necessary expeditions from the house, I managed to lay my hands on a number of different-sized sandglasses, whose steady and visible changes seemed to have a comforting influence on her while I was away. Whereas clocks offered no reassurance to her, because their largely unchanging faces provided no record of how much time had passed (and just as little indication of how much was still to come), I could set up the largest sandglass, which ran for just under an hour, and leave her engrossed in its silent, trustworthy demonstration of the flow of time until my return. Provided she saw me again before the trickle of sand reached its end, she remained unconcerned by my absence.

117

25

ST AUGUSTINE WROTE IN HIS *CONFESSIONS*, 'WHAT, THEN, IS TIME? If no one asks of me, I know; if I wish to explain to him who asks, I know not . . . My soul yearns to know this most entangled enigma.' Since when (and he died in AD 430), nobody has come up with much in the way of an answer to his question, least of all our twentieth-century physicists with their glib talk of space–time, that shifty accounting device of cosmological commerce.

What really perplexed Augustine were the apparent differences in nature between the past, the present and the future. His view was, roughly speaking, that the present is the only thing that is real, that exists, and that both the past and the future exist only in the present. The past is memory, which happens in the present, and the future is anticipation, which also happens in the present. As he puts it, there are three times, 'a present of things past, a present of things present, and a present of things future': 'The present of things past is memory, the present of things present is sight, and the present of things future is expectation.'

But far and away the most intriguing of his conclusions,

certainly for a watchmaker, is his recognition (obvious after you've heard it) that time can be measured only while it is passing. We cannot measure how long a past event lasted and equally we cannot measure how long a future event, even if we could foresee it, will last. We can make deductions about past duration. We can say that, if we knew the size of the apple, the temperature of the air and the distance it dropped before hitting Newton's head, we could determine how long it took to fall, but we cannot possibly go back to check our reckoning through measurement, any more than we can *measure* the time between now and next Christmas. And if time is not susceptible to measurement in either the past or the future, then in what sense can it possibly be said to exist in either?

To believe in a time past, you have to believe that time is something real, something objective, something to do with 'what's out there', and there are indeed people who do believe in an objective past. People who imagine the present moment as the front edge of an eternally advancing flow, like a never-diminishing bolt of universal fabric unrolling across a dark and endless floor. For them, time past is real in the sense that it has existed and continues to exist in our memories, unlike time future, which we can only imagine; and, since they also believe (without any good evidence) that memory and imagination are in some way different, so the past and the future seem different to them.

The contrary position, held by proponents of the *block universe view*, proposes time to be something entirely subjective. Just as what we mean by 'here' is simply where we believe we are, so what we mean by 'now' is *when* we believe we are. But, although we have some degree of apparent control over *where* we are – we can choose to stroll down to the pub or fly to Kuala Lumpur – we do not intuitively feel that we could ever have the same freedom to decide *when* we are.

It is as though we are travelling on a moving train in which all the seats face away from the engine, so that we see only the landscape we have passed through and not that which lies ahead. For some reason we are prevented from turning round to see where we are going. To adopt Augustine's stance is to believe that there *is* no landscape up ahead, only our expectation of it, just as the landscape which has disappeared from view behind us exists only in our memory. The only things that are real are those we can see out of the window at the moment of passing, things which we experience in the present.

But are we correct in so casually referring to this as the present? By the time we notice something in the landscape – a cow, say – the moment has passed. It takes some measurable time – not much, but some – for the light from the cow to reach our eyes, just as it takes time for the chemicals and electrons in our brains to produce in us a conscious awareness of the cow's form. If there is a gap, however brief, between perception and conscious awareness, then we can experience nothing in the present. The most we can say is that 'the present moment' is the name we give to our most recent memories, and it is no more or less real than any of our other memories.

In the block universe, the landscape is still there after we have passed, and further up the line lies scenery which is always there, whether we reach it or not. Here once more, as with the apparent motion of a clock's hands, we should be aware of the purely relative nature of the changes we experience. For all we can know, the carriage in which we appear to travel may be stationary and it is the landscape which moves, as in those old film sets of train compartments with endlessly revolving soft-focus backgrounds, repeating themselves behind the foreground actors (and who is to say that our own universal landscape will not one day repeat itself?). Or perhaps both elements are moving in different directions, so that, as we and our train of thought move forward, the universe rushes to meet us, and we live our whole lives backing into a steady headwind of future events.

26

THEN THE WORDS BEGAN TO GO. ONE MORNING THE FOLLOWING June, after her morning bath, Elizabeth called to me from the bedroom with the voice of a stranger, a wavering, high-pitched wail underscored with barely controlled dread. I found her perched on the window seat, wrapped in her dressing-gown, darting nervous, suspicious glances around the room.

'There are no rabbits,' she wailed. 'What have you done with all the rabbits? I must see them, I must see them now, I always feed them at this time of day, you know that, so why have you taken them away?'

'Which rabbits?' I asked her. 'I don't remember any rabbits.'

'Yes you do, you do,' she screamed, 'every morning after my bath . . . have I had my bath?'

'Yes, you have.'

'Well, then. Where are the rabbits?'

There were no rabbits. We had never kept rabbits. All I could think was that somehow she had become confused in her mind about some aspect of her daily routine. I picked up her hairbrush from the dressing table and held it out to her, but she batted it angrily from my hand. I hunted around and found her handbag under the bed where she must have kicked it. Her eyes widened and she clapped her hands together and held them out for the bag.

'There they are,' she cooed. 'There they all are, aren't they?' And she calmly busied herself applying her makeup, shooting petulant glances in my direction and cooing to herself, 'There they are, there they are . . .'

These periods of verbal confusion came and went. Some days were worse than others. On occasion there could even be an eerie, almost poetic felicity to the expressions she chose, as when she peremptorily announced, 'We must change all the light bulbs', and it took her fifteen minutes of shouting and gesticulating to make me understand that what she really wanted was for me to deadhead the roses. At other times there would be no readily discernible link between what she said and what she meant. The day she warned me 'There are rats in the car' was a particularly difficult one. What she meant to tell me – and this emerged only after a great deal of weeping, spitting, fury and frustration on both sides – was that the ivy on the side of the house was beginning to encroach into the guttering.

'The fire threw the bird into the clouds,' she whispered to me one misty morning as I was cooking breakfast for us in the kitchen. I smiled and poured her a glass of grapefruit juice. As I handed it to her she clamped her fingers around my wrist and, placing her lips close enough to my ear for me to feel the warmth of her breath, hissed, 'Yesterday. The fire, the dead black fire, blew the bird up the smoke tunnel into the heavens above.'

'How strange,' I said.

'It was.' She nodded, glancing over to the old fireplace. 'Very strange. And very frightening, too.'

'And this happened . . . yesterday?'

'Yesterday afternoon. The black cloud, the dust gathering to surround the poor bird, to stifle it, to thrust it up into the cold, cold sky.'

Two days later, as she and I sat drinking tea in the kitchen, listening to the afternoon short story on the radio, a starling fell down the chimney into the fireplace, hurling forth a dense dark billow of soot and ashes. I managed to grab the half-stunned, feebly flapping creature and carry it to the back door, where I set it down on the top step. Waiting for it to recover, I became aware of Elizabeth standing very still beside me, smiling down at the wretched creature.

'Hello, birdie,' she said quietly. 'We weren't expecting you till tomorrow.'

27

SINCE BREGUET'S INVENTION OF THE TOURBILLON, IT HAS BEEN axiomatic with watchmakers that a spring-detent chronometer escapement, in conjunction with a one-minute tourbillon, will furnish a mechanical watch with the highest-attainable degree of accuracy, and so naturally this was the combination I selected for my movement. Such a mechanism, however, has one severe drawback for practical purposes. It is very delicate, and any sudden twist of the watch will cause the escapement to 'set', or stop. A similar action can restart the watch but can also 'trip' the movement so that the balance operates too quickly, releasing the escapement twice every two swings instead of once, which makes the watch run at double its correct speed until the oscillations settle down again.

Much ingenious work has been done, continuing well into the twentieth century, to cure this fault, but the general view has come to be that such instruments are best left undisturbed by motion, preferably lying on their backs. In this position, of course, there is no advantage to having a tourbillon at all. (Similarly, there is continuing argument as to what contribution a tourbillon can be expected to make to the accuracy of a wristwatch – the current Breguet range offers a number of elegant examples – considering that the position of a watch worn on the wrist is constantly changing, unlike a pocket watch, which tends to remain in the 'pendant-down' or upright position when carried on the person.)

Breguet himself, for reasons of practicality, settled for a lever escapement, which acts on the notched 'scape wheel rather like the two claws of a crab. In a sort of swivelling horizontal rocking motion, the crab allows the wheel to rotate by alternately releasing one notch with its left claw (or pallet) and catching another with its right. Since I had no intention of subjecting the watch to any rough handling, my single-minded pursuit of accuracy determined that I employ the chronometer escapement, particularly so because the making of a spring detent is among the most challenging tasks a watchmaker can undertake.

Without prevailing overly on your patience by describing the entire process, I may perhaps offer some indication of the difficulties involved by describing how just one tiny part of the escapement is manufactured. To make the spring which gives the device its name you must begin with a short, thin ribbon of low-carat gold (anything richer than nine-carat is too soft) which has first to be annealed and then hammered on a perfectly smooth block of hard steel, reducing its overall thickness to about five-thousandths of an inch. This is the rough, preparatory work. To reduce its thickness further you must rest it on a flat piece of willow and rub it with Water-of-

Ayr Stone, dampened with oil, until its thickness is reduced by more than half, to two-thousandths of an inch. Any incautious or inattentive stroke at this stage will kink the spring, or even break it, and you will have to begin all over again.

For the final thinning and finishing you must use oil and oilstone dust, applied with a flat steel polisher, which unless you keep it perfectly square to the surface of the spring will rub away one side more than the other, rendering the spring useless. If all is still well, the spring can either be polished, with a zinc polisher and diamantine, or grained using a strip of ivory and dry emery (triple-washed). The final result will be a perfectly uniform strip of glittering gold, many times thinner than a human hair. In the end it took me a total of eighty-three hours, spread over two weeks, to produce a spring in which I could place sufficient confidence to encourage me to proceed with the rest of the work. Along the way I had rejected and discarded, for one reason or another, eleven previous attempts.

28

IT WAS CHARLOTTE'S VISIT THAT PRECIPITATED THE FINAL DESCENT INTO tumult and confusion. She arrived by taxi one Friday afternoon that August, hefting an enormous soft tote bag, and the expression on my face must have betrayed my surprise at seeing her.

'Oh, my God,' she said, paying off the cab driver. 'She didn't tell you I was coming, did she?'

'No,' was all I could say.

'Shit. Shit and derision.'

'Not that it isn't nice to see you.'

She peered into my face. 'You look pretty ghastly,' she said as I bent down to pick up the bag. Below a white broderie anglaise blouse with a wide scoop neck she was wearing thin cotton culottes from which her naked brown legs descended with the sturdiness of sycamores.

I followed her inside and called upstairs to Elizabeth, 'Lizzie, look who's come to see us.'

The moment Elizabeth appeared on the landing the irrepressible Charlotte flung wide her arms and hooted, 'So this is your little rustic retreat, poppet. It's absolutely gorgeous. I mean, what a joke place.'

Elizabeth frowned at her and slowly began to descend the stairs.

'Lizzie,' I told her gently, 'Charlotte has come to stay with us for . . . a while.'

'Just for the weekend, poppet, like we agreed.'

Elizabeth's expression showed no sign of having agreed any such thing, nor any hint of recognition, much less welcome. Her darting gaze, skipping from Charlotte's face to mine, then back upstairs as though seeking a route for flight, reflected nothing but the all too familiar panic and bewilderment which was steadily taking over her life.

Charlotte climbed the stairs to meet her and enfolded her in those two meaty arms. Elizabeth suffered the smothering embrace as might a condescending family cat, not fighting against it but waiting with incurious good nature to be released. Only her unblinking eyes locked on mine over Charlotte's shoulder, struggled to express some inner appeal.

'Charlotte,' I said, 'perhaps you and Lizzie could go up and sort out your room.'

And then occurred one of those strange quirks of the disease, an unexpected interlude of lucidity, as though the flow of thought had found a new path through the crumbling brain tissue, like a blocked underground stream bubbling its way up into the sunlight.

'Of course,' said Elizabeth, wriggling free of the stifling hug, her eyes now bright and alive. 'Let's get you settled in,

Charlotte.' She turned back to me. 'Which room did we think Charlotte would like?'

'Perhaps the yellow room at the end,' I ventured.

Elizabeth clapped her hands and squealed, 'You'll love it, Charlotte, you'll absolutely love it. It's like waking up right in the middle of a sunflower.'

'Sounds wild,' Charlotte responded, with a backward glance to me that was not without its own mute appeal.

'Keep an eye on Lizzie for me,' I said to her. 'I'll need to fetch some supplies from the village.'

'Don't go mad on my account. Simple country fare is all I crave.'

'How's Malcolm?' I called after her as the pair of them disappeared upstairs.

'Fuck knows,' Charlotte hooted from above.

That evening I prepared us a late supper of home-cured ham and local farmhouse cheeses, and a big bowl of pasta salad with fresh broad beans. Charlotte, who had drunk a whole bottle of Rosé de Provence before we sat down at the table, was on exhaustingly buoyant form. Malcolm, it appeared, had finally taken one too many sherbets with a client and Charlotte had thrown him out. Physically, I suspected.

'You mean . . . for ever?' Elizabeth asked, wide-eyed.

'I fear not,' panted Charlotte, wrestling with a corkscrew and a second bottle of chilled rosé, which she had clamped unflinchingly between her bare thighs. 'I shall probably take the little weasel back again. I always do. Thing is, he's so useful around the house. You know, shelves and things.'

130

'Will you still go to bed together?' asked Elizabeth.

'Sex, you mean? With Malcolm? That was all over years ago, poppet. I mean, have you smelled his breath? Heaven forfend. No, I have the sweetest little electrician in Muswell Hill who looks after all that. I picked him up when he came to rewire the basement. He's absolutely terrified of me – does exactly what I tell him, like a slave. It's marvellous.'

Elizabeth looked down at her plate, smiled and said, 'Robert and I share a bed, don't we? When I'm not doing my walking. I have such a lot of walking to do, don't I, Robert?'

'Yes, lots of walking,' I said.

'And there's my tapestry, of course,' she went on. 'That takes up a fair amount of time, I can tell you. I must show it to you.' She sprang up from the table and ran off upstairs.

It had grown dark as we talked, so I lit candles.

Charlotte refilled her glass, sucked up a long, noisy mouthful and said, 'I had no idea she was this ill. She sounded perfectly all right on the phone.'

'Sometimes she does,' I told her.

'But when I arrived she didn't seem to recognize me. Didn't have the foggiest idea who I was.'

'Some days she doesn't even recognize me.'

'I had no idea. Are they treating her at all?'

'Not really. Nobody knows what causes it, so they're a bit stuck when it comes to treatment. To begin with I read a lot about it, everything I could lay my hands on, but the picture gets very confused. One group of researchers thinks it's

131

connected with some protein in the brain, another group seems to believe that the problem is in the synapses. Some of them are convinced it's a genetic thing. Nobody really knows.'

'But they might come up with a cure?'

'Not in time, I'm afraid.'

'Jesus, how long are we talking about?'

'I honestly don't know. She's started to deteriorate pretty rapidly of late.'

'But what – weeks, months?'

'A year, maybe. Perhaps less.'

'Let's hope it's as long as can be,' she said, taking both my hands in hers, and I acknowledged to myself at that moment, with a rush of revulsion, of near nausea, that this was not a hope I shared.

People say that there is nothing more cruelly wounding to the heart than the loss of one's own child. I do not know that pain, nor is it likely that I ever shall. Except that it seems to me that all children are bound to lose themselves through the simple expedient of growing into adulthood, and I believe that I have sometimes detected in parents a kind of grieving for the baby that has been smothered for ever by the child it has become, just as the child is consumed by the adolescent, never to reappear. But the child does not really die. He persists, concealed within the thing into which he has turned, not intact like in a Russian doll – identical, only smaller – but in there somewhere, at least in part, as the person he always was. As the memories and the memory of the person he never ceased to be.

But with Elizabeth, as the memory continued to fail, the person inside would fade away. Hers was fated to be (I had read enough by then to know) a kind of inside-out death, not like dying from heart disease or cancer where the body conspires to starve the brain of oxygen, but a betrayal of the body by the brain, as it forgets how to operate the fleshly mechanism, first sending it untrustworthy messages, then no messages at all, abandoning it to its own devices.

Just over three years had passed since that first amnesic episode. Would I truly want her condemned to further long years of deterioration? Many a husband wishes his wife dead after he has ceased to love her and she has ceased to be the grudgingly acquiescent sump for his lust, has become instead a barely supportable irritation, a nettle for his nerves, a siphon on his means. But here was I wishing Elizabeth dead sooner rather than later not because I did not love her but because I did, I still did, in spite of the fact that she had long ago changed from being recognizably the person I had first loved. Or was it for my own future that I feared? Was it my shameful reluctance to stay by her as she fell apart that I was beginning to sense? Was it the bald fact that I did not trust myself to cope, did not trust myself to *want* to cope?

When Elizabeth reappeared, clutching the tapestry frame, her sewing basket tucked under her arm, I could tell at once that there had been some change, some new mental landslip even in the short time since she had been gone. She stood in the candlelight, framed by the kitchen doorway, seeming to smile at the two of us, although the lucid moment had passed and her eyes were focused far beyond where we sat, Charlotte still squeezing my hands in hers.

Elizabeth walked slowly over to us, carefully set down the half-finished tapestry and began rummaging in her basket. Charlotte released my hands, sliding hers away, palms flat to the table, and reached again for her glass. As she leaned forward Elizabeth swivelled round, her raised hand describing a twinkling chromium arc through the air on its way to plunging her sewing scissors into Charlotte's neck.

For a palpable moment nothing moved, everything was frozen, candlelit like a painting by Georges de La Tour – Charlotte's glass half-raised to a mouth which had become a perfectly circular black disc, my own hands half-extended across the table towards a calmly smiling Elizabeth, who looked for all the world as though she were momentarily resting an affectionate sisterly hand on the other woman's shoulder. Then came the blood, not spurting – no artery had been breached, thank God – but oozing, slow and dark, pooling momentarily in the hollow above Charlotte's collarbone before spilling over to roll down into the white cotton tracery of her blouse. It was not a scream she made; more a tremulous whimper of disbelief and indignation. Elizabeth backed away still smiling, leaving the scissors embedded, their twin finger-holes glimmering like the eye-rims of some leering incubus squatting on Charlotte's shoulder.

After that the night was filled with flashing blue lights and ambulances and stitches in a deserted, echoing casualty department somewhere and awkward questions from the police, and at the end of it all Elizabeth, ever-smiling, entrusted to the uncertain mercies of the local hospital's secure mental ward. It was the start of the really bad time.

29

THE MOST DURABLY ACCURATE OF ALL TERRESTRIAL TIMEPIECES, OR
at any rate a good example of it, can be found in Oxford under
the custodianship of that city's Museum of the History of
Science. Known by horologists simply as the Horizontal
Instrument, this particular version was made in 1635, taking
the form of a circular brass plate, eighteen inches in diameter
and densely engraved, but with no moving parts. (It had one
movable part, a pivoted rule to assist in taking readings, but it
possessed nothing in the way of clockwork.) It was a stereo-
graphic projection of the heavens, of the celestial sphere, onto
the plane of the user's horizon, with the centre of the disc
corresponding to the zenith above the observer's head. The
finely engraved horizontal lines indicated the positions of the
equator and the tropics, the Meridian line and the ecliptic; the
vertical arcs radiating from a point below the zenith marked
the hours of the day. Although the mathematics of its conception and the intricacy of its construction were both highly
sophisticated, the instrument itself was delightfully easy to
use.

To its seventeenth-century public, a public fascinated by

the behaviour of the natural world but for the most part unable to perform all but the simplest tasks of multiplication and division, the device's principal charm lay in its effortless ability to predict the precise position of the sun at any time of any day. By inserting a pin into the central hole perpendicular to the face and suspending the instrument vertically with its edge towards the sun, the sun's altitude could be read from the point where the pin's shadow crossed the degree scale. The rule (the movable part) could then be rotated on its pivot at the zenith point to align one of the almucantars – the lines of equal altitude – with the day of the year, and the true position of the sun in the heavens (and, by inference, the time) could be read from the dial.

The individual most credibly identified with the invention of this ingenious instrument is William Oughtred, who was born in Eton around 1575 and went up to King's College, Cambridge on 1st September, 1592. Here he spent the next eleven years, eventually becoming a Fellow. Later, after he was installed in London by his patron, the Earl of Arundel, he taught mathematics, particularly algebra, to all who came, and charged nothing for his tuition (Christopher Wren was one of his pupils). He also seems to have been happy to provide designs for the London instrument-maker Elias Allen, which the latter could sell for a hefty profit to a gentry thirsting for scientific novelty.

In 1628, his genial nature notwithstanding, Oughtred was drawn into an acrimonious squabble with a blustering rogue named Richard Delamain, who, it appeared, had caught sight of the partly completed Horizontal Instrument at Elias Allen's workshop and had borrowed Oughtred's letter of instruction to the engraver, keeping it for two weeks – plenty of time in which to make a detailed copy. He converted the projection into a quadrant by the simple trick of folding the original in half, and then secretly commissioned one of Allen's assistants to make the instrument for him in brass (this version, too, can be seen in Oxford).

Accused by Oughtred of plagiarism, the wretched Delamain plunged into a frenzied and bombastic counter-attack, prompting one of his acquaintances to marvel at the indiscretion of a man 'who being conscious to himself that he is but the pickpurse of another man's wit, would thus inconsiderately provoke and awake a sleeping Lion'. But, if Oughtred was that lion, he appears to have been a generally good-natured one, and in the course of time it emerged that he had long before given away two examples of the instrument as gifts, one at least thirty years previously to the Bishop of Winchester and one in 1608 to a local lady of his acquaintance who had expressed an interest in mathematics.

The thing itself is, to my eyes, an object of ferocious beauty, not in the same way that a painting or a rose may be considered beautiful, but more in the way that a mathematical equation can be beautiful. There is a kind of glorious *rightness* to it. This pitted and grubby disc of brass proclaims an unwavering conviction that this is the way things are, where they are and where they will always be. It tells the truth, as its maker saw it.

When I was at Cambridge I liked to think of Oughtred in the college, treading the same paths that I had come to walk more than three hundred and fifty years later. In my mind's eye I saw him sitting in the chapel (in his day, a 'modern' building still less than fifty years old), surrounded by those soaring perpendicular effusions, his upturned face dappled by the multicoloured shafts of sunlight pouring in through the stained glass, as the inner eye of his imagination focused not on the contrived human artifice of the fan-vaulted ceiling but on the divinely ordained order which he could envisage in the celestial bowl beyond.

In the form of a double horizontal dial, like the example in the London Science Museum, also engraved by Elias Allen, the projection works in conjunction with an upright gnomon like that of a regular sundial; and, as with all sundials, it is self-correcting. The earth is its clockwork, its moving part, and, as the earth slows in its rotation, the dial continues to define an hour as one twenty-fourth of however long the planet takes to turn. Had the Parisian atomic clock been running since William Oughtred's undergraduate days, we should find that its reading would by now be as much as five minutes adrift from that of the Horizontal Instrument. As far as the planet and all its doings are concerned, the clock would be five minutes 'fast'.

If we are to respect the earth in this way as a natural timekeeper, by contrast with our man-made instruments, we will also be forced to acknowledge one of the universe's other natural timekeepers, the pulsar known as PSR 1913 + 16.

Not only does this remote neutron star revolve around its companion star at a tremendous velocity – sometimes achieving one-tenth of the speed of light – it is also rotating at high speed on its axis. Its entire 'day' is only 0.059 seconds long. The beam of radiation, which is emitted from the surface of this spinning neutron star, reaches us in regular pulses, like the beam from a distant lighthouse. Such pulsars are the most accurate known 'clocks' in the universe, accurate to seventy-five-millionths of a second over the course of a year. But we are still prompted to ask, 'As measured by what?' Our caesium clock? The one that flew to America, or the one that stayed at home?

Not that many months ago, in a restaurant in Switzerland, I learned how, by taking additional measurements of other binary pulsars and by comparing the readings not just against our terrestrial atomic clocks but against each other, we are about to achieve the next major step forward in time measurement.

What time will it be *then*? We may find that it adds little to the comfort and security of our lives on this planet to know. Just as the priests of Islam had no use for the mechanical division of the day into equal hours, so we may find that the establishment of pulsar time will be of little practical use to us. It will not tell us when midday on our world occurs with even the accuracy of Oughtred's disc of brass.

Slowly, inevitably, like the atomic clock in Paris, this far-distant convocation of neutron stars will find itself out of step with the time in which and through which we live, and when this happens we shall find that we cannot adjust the pulsars as we can the atomic clock, and, as we cannot make the world spin any faster, so the two will be irreconcilable. We may at last come to wonder in our confusion and frustration whether there may not be any such thing as time at all.

30

THEY HAD SEDATED HER, THEY TOLD ME WHEN I ARRIVED AT THE
hospital the following afternoon. They had also strapped
her into her bed, which they did not tell me. Broad rubber
webbing clasped her arms to the raised sides of the metal
cot. Her eyes were closed and it was impossible to tell if
she were asleep or in some kind of narcotic stupor. They
had put her in a small secure side ward whose solid door
bore one small window of thick wired glass, and an
electronic lock, into which the ward sister tapped a combination with practised nonchalance. There were four beds
in the ward, the other three occupied by sleeping women
of evidently great age. None of the others had been
strapped in. The ward sister, a small freckled creature with
brick-red hair and a sharply pointed nose like a puppet's,
stood beside me at the foot of the bed and whispered, 'She
passed a very peaceful night. What there was left of it.' She
sounded Irish.

'Why is she strapped in?' I whispered back.

'So that she doesn't hurt herself.'

'Or anyone else?'

'There's very little risk of that. Not on the medication which has been prescribed for her.'

'So what happens now?' I was conscious of my whisper coarsening and increasing in volume. 'Are you going to keep her asleep for the rest of her life?'

'I think you had better have a little talk with the doctor,' she said. 'Sit yourself down here and he'll be along presently.' She pulled the curtains around the bed. They made a noise on their rails like gentle surf breaking on shingle.

I sat down on the small plastic-covered stacking chair by the bedside and looked at Elizabeth. They had dressed her in a thin white cotton gown and her bare arms were red where the rubber had chafed them. Her breathing seemed impossibly slow and shallow and, when I tried to match my own to its rhythm, I could manage only four or five breaths before I was forced to fill my lungs with the lifeless, overheated hospital air. I took one of her hands in mine, but it was cold and unresponsive. I rested my forehead on the hard steel bed-frame, closed my eyes and whimpered like a dog having a bad dream.

The curtain rustled behind me and a figure in a white coat slid through the gap. He seemed young for a doctor – a houseman, I guessed. He had the build of a rugby forward and the physiognomy of a bored bus driver.

'Mr Garrett?' he asked, extending his hand to me. His grasp was predictably resolute. 'My name's Bennett. Registrar.' He nodded in Elizabeth's direction. 'Your wife, is it not?'

'It is – she is – my wife.'

'I gather from the notes that were taken last night that she had previously been diagnosed as suffering from dementia.'

'That's right.'

'And there was some kind of an incident yesterday evening?'

'She stabbed a friend of ours with a pair of scissors.'

'Has she ever done anything like that before?'

'No. She's not at all a violent person.'

'It sounds like what we call a catastrophic reaction. Which is not to say that it's a catastrophe in the usual sense of the word, although I suppose in this case it could easily have turned out that way. Was the friend badly injured?'

'I don't believe so. She seemed more shocked than hurt.'

'You see, what it is . . . people whose brains have gone a bit, you know . . . wonky . . . sometimes overreact wildly to situations, largely because they can't understand what's happening. They panic, d'you see? Panic. It could well be that your wife mistook your friend for someone else, or perhaps she saw her as some sort of a threat.' He had slipped into that tone and mode of speech the medical profession sometimes uses to address the laity and which the rest of us reserve for our less bright domestic animals.

I said, 'How long will you need to keep her here?'

'Do you want us to keep her here?'

'No. I want her to come home.'

'Good, good. Well, that's splendid news. What it is, d'you see, we don't need to keep her here at all. Frankly, we need the bed. She's not sick, I mean, or yes, rather, she is sick, but not

144

with anything we can cure, d'you see? If she had TB, say, or a broken hip, then of course she'd have to stay.'

'What if she does something like it again?'

'The medication will take care of that. As long as you're on hand to make sure she takes it.'

'What kind of medication?'

'Pills, pills. Something to calm her down, stop the panic. It's the panic that triggers it off, d'you see? Triggers off the overreaction. How's she been sleeping?'

'Not well. Some nights, not at all.'

'Pacing about, wandering?' Then, in answer to my nod: 'Usual pattern, by the sound of it. We can let you have some sleepy pills, too.'

'Forgive me,' I asked him, 'but did you just say "sleepy pills"?'

'Yep. Sleepy pills.'

A crimson flush suffused his ears and he was overcome by a pressing need to rearrange his stethoscope.

'I'll see about those prescriptions,' he said. 'Stay as long as you like.'

When he had gone I asked the staff nurse to leave the curtains drawn around the bed while I waited for Elizabeth to awaken. From time to time I could hear sounds of activity in the ward outside, the squeak of trolley wheels on linoleum, the rattle of instruments and metal bowls, brief murmured consultations and once a muffled cry of unidentifiable anguish. After two hours and seven minutes another nurse, who had come to take readings for Elizabeth's charts, offered me a cup of tea, which I declined. I have no recollection of what she looked like.

After another forty-five minutes I had the sister release me from the ward and found a payphone on the stairs, from which I was able to call Charlotte's number. She was already back home, her wound having been satisfactorily treated by the casualty department.

'They described it as "nasty but not life-threatening",' she related with a snort. 'They seemed more worried about tetanus than anything else. How's Lizzie doing?'

'Spark out. They've strapped her into a bed and pumped her full of sedatives.'

'I can't tell you how awful I feel about all this. It was really stupid of me to come without talking to you first. Serves me right.'

'Charlotte,' I said, 'you can't blame yourself for getting stabbed. I'm the one that should be apologizing, but I had really no idea she could get violent.'

'Look out for yourself, poppet,' she said. 'And let me know if there's anything I can do.'

At five minutes to ten, just as the light outside was fading, I returned to the ward to find Elizabeth moving her feet beneath the bedclothes, firstly as a spasmodic twitching but rapidly building to a rhythmic walking movement. Her hands started to flap and her arms strained against the restraints. Her eyes were still closed but it was obvious that the whole of her body was straining to be off walking, wandering somewhere. I pressed the alarm buzzer, which

146

had been pointed out to me by the ward sister, and within one minute Bennett reappeared with a staff nurse and gave Elizabeth an injection in the arm. Within three minutes her wild thrashing had subsided once more into immobility.

Bennett unhooked the clipboard chart from the foot of the bed, glanced at it and said, 'I think we'll need a couple of days to get the balance right. Some of these drugs are pretty tricky customers in combination, dosages not easy to work out, d'you see? What we want is to minimize any nasty old side-effects, don't we? She'll be asleep for about twelve hours now, so I should go home and get yourself a good night's rest. Need anything yourself to help you sleep?'

I shook my head. 'No sleepy pills, thank you,' I told him.

'Fair enough,' he said airily, and off he went.

31

HOW DO WE KNOW THE SEQUENCE OF OUR EXPERIENCES? WHAT gives us the sense that one incident in our past happened before another? Are our memories laid down somewhere in our brains in chronological order, stacked in the recesses of our minds, the oldest at the bottom, like a pile of fading magazines we never quite got round to clearing out? If so, how would we manage to retrieve them? To put a name to, say, the distantly remembered face of a childhood friend we should have to know the exact time and date when we committed it to memory. Yet our identification of that moment would be possible only if we first recalled the very detail which defined the occasion. We would only know where to look after finding the thing we were looking for.

Imagine the mind as a library where the books are memories, arranged on the shelves not according to subject matter or any alphabetical system but simply in the order in which they were acquired. It would be a long and tedious task to locate any specific volume, but, having found it, you would at least know which books preceded its arrival and which were added later. Something in the way we commit our experiences to memory must give us this sense of sequence, this fundamental awareness of 'before' and 'after'.

Suppose the rules of the library dictated that every time a book were taken from a shelf it had to be replaced not in its original position but right at the end, with the newest volumes, because it would now be a new edition of a previous one. Every time we retrieve a memory do we remember the remembering? And what becomes of the old memory – is there now a gap on the shelf? This would mean that every memory would make us feel as though its related event had only just occurred. All our memories would become new, simply through the act of retrieval. The chronology would become jumbled, our judgement of 'before' and 'after' would become unsound and our belief in sequentiality unsustainable.

It seems as though the library dictates that, once a volume has been taken from the shelf and examined, it must be replaced in its former position and then rewritten before being added in a re-created form to the shelf of current acquisitions. In this way, we experience new memories of old events as well as old memories of old events. So it is that, every time we call to mind an event or relate some much-retold episode, each accretion of narrative embroidery and every small inaccuracy becomes compounded in the recollection. We are not just the repositories of our memories; we are their authors. In terms of process, there is no detectable difference between memory and imagination.

These are the thoughts which occurred to me as I began the

task of creating hands for the watch. I had elected quite early on to base the design of the face on Patek Philippe's gold hunter chronograph No. 94 189, sold on 20th February, 1897, with its white enamel dial, Roman numerals and the winding crown at the three o'clock position. Although I did not propose incorporating the instrument's chronographic (stop watch) function, I intended retaining the long sweep second hand to provide a clearer reading against minute divisions, subdivided into five.

For this reason, I could dispense with the small seconds dial at the six o'clock position, replacing it with a circular window through which the operation of the tourbillon could be seen. This was, I must admit, purely an aesthetic decision on my part – a tourbillon will work perfectly satisfactorily in the dark – but anyone who has witnessed the mechanism in motion will testify to the mesmeric fascination it exerts upon the observer.

The design of the hands also demanded a degree of modification. The hunter has been described as having Breguet hands of blued steel, and the 'blued steel' part is correct. But the minute and the hour hands are heavy, bloated travesties of Breguet's original conception. He himself was no less preoccupied by the design of his watch hands than by that of any other part of the mechanism, partly because of his tireless pursuit of mechanical elegance but also as an acknowledgement that the humble hands perform a vital, if obvious, function: they tell us the time.

He originally favoured gold hands in the English style (he

was a great admirer of the English), until around 1783, when he created a new style of hand, made from either gold or blued steel, comprising a long, slender stem leading from the centre of the face to a hollow disc, eccentrically pierced towards the outer rim, and beyond that a short point. The pierced disc, known as either an 'apple' or a 'crescent moon', became as firmly associated with his name as did the Breguet overcoil, and was widely adopted by watchmakers until almost the end of the nineteenth century, by which time even the Breguet company had abandoned it, reviving the design only in the early 1930s.

Although many fine old Swiss movements have nut-brown screw heads, for instance, English makers have always preferred their steel to be blue, and perhaps it was from this that Breguet took his inspiration. The blueing of steel is a process which, while straightforward, nevertheless requires a degree of vigilance. The hands must first be hardened and tempered and then polished with diamantine (used wet rather than dry), and all traces of oil or grease must be removed. To keep it flat, the hand is laid on a brass block that has been drilled with a hole to provide a recess for the raised boss. As the block is heated, the colour of the steel passes through a series of changes from light straw through dark straw (the colour of Elizabeth's hair), brown, purple and finally to deep blue. The skill lies in knowing the precise moment to remove the heat so as to retain the merest ghost of purple within the final blue.

Having neither the facilities nor the skill for enamelling the face, I machine-engraved the design with a modified wheel

151

cutter on a disc of sterling silver, which also allowed me to mark the divisions with finer lines than could have been achieved by the use of enamel or paint. This also provided me with the opportunity to adorn the face with that most exquisite of all Breguet's decorative innovations, *guillochage*, the engraving (either by machine or, in the rarer pieces, by hand) of tiny, repetitive patterns across the whole face of the watch, interrupted by circular bands of concentrically polished metal bearing the numerals and divisions. The technique, though not invented by Breguet, was first used by him on watch faces as a means of increasing the legibility of the various indicators, and certainly the multi-directional reflections thrown up by the finely worked silver render the face comfortably readable from even the most oblique angle. It took me seven weeks to complete the face and hands to my satisfaction.

The reason my thoughts strayed to considerations of sequentiality while fitting the hands was that in adjusting their different positions against the face I was causing the indicated time to move backwards and forwards in random hops and skips, one moment reading two twenty-three, say, the next nine fifty-one. It was I, not the watch, who determined the order in which these readings might be taken (the watch had no say in the matter, not having been wound).

I was the cause and the readings were the effect, but, as I moved the hands haphazardly around the dial, what was it that told me that the readings were not in any sensible order? What internal mechanism of mind continued to inform me that a quarter past three was not mere seconds away from twenty-five to eight; and, if I chanced to move the hands backwards five minutes, what was it that told me I had contrived the 'later' reading before the 'earlier' one?

I began to feel that queasy sense of dislocation attendant on Hume's theory that 'cause' and 'effect' are simply different expressions for 'before' and 'after'; that when two events invariably appear related, it is only force of habit (or superstition, as Wittgenstein was to insist) that makes us refer to the preceding event as the cause and the later event as the effect.

In an earlier attempt to break free from this habit of thought, Arnold Geulincx, a disciple of Descartes, had come up with his now famous theory of 'two clocks'. He supposed the existence of two clocks, both of which kept perfect time (he and Einstein might have spent an interesting few hours discussing the implications); whenever one of the clocks indicated the hour, the other would strike, so that if you saw the one and heard the other you might conclude that the one had caused the other to strike. His purpose in pursuing this line of thought was to show that the mind and the body could be operating independently of one another and that volition was only an apparent fact. Raising a wine glass to your lips may feel like a voluntary act but in reality, Geulincx implied, your body is acting entirely on its own and the fact that it may be doing what you want it to do is just a happy coincidence. As a theory, it has an agreeable daftness to it and is surprisingly tricky to argue against.

The theory was perhaps being echoed by Abram-Louis Breguet in 1795 when, it is thought, he first conceived his *sympathique* timepieces. These truly extraordinary instruments comprised two elements: a chronometer in a glass case, and a watch that could be slotted into a recess on top of the case. The watch was carried about during the day like a normal timepiece, but overnight in its recess, apparently by mere proximity to the clock, it would 'magically' correct itself, so that each morning the two readings would be found precisely to coincide, as though in sympathy with one another. It was a highly ingenious and complicated mechanism and he only ever sold five – all of them to kings or princes. (The *sympathique* clock No. 666 and its watch No. 721 remain in the royal collection at Buckingham Palace.) After the death of Abram-Louis, an inspired new refinement was added by Louis-Clément Breguet in the form of a winding function, which meant that not only would the owner find his watch corrected in the morning, he would also find it fully wound. The mechanism by which this was achieved was not fully understood at the time and it is easy to see how its mysteries might have given rise to speculation about cause and effect at a distance.

Even though we have come to believe that one event somehow *makes* another happen, we are only comfortable believing it in one direction. If by some clumsy movement of an elbow we accidentally knock that same wine glass off the table to shatter on the floor below, we feel that we have caused the breakage. We find it disquieting to suppose that it might be the glass that moved our elbow, the shards somehow reassembling themselves into a whole glass before levitating to the tabletop in order to cause the offending elbow to adopt a different position.

If we record the event on film we can run it in either direction, but when we run it backwards our memory of the event (and all similar events) tells us that what we are seeing is wrong. A later event simply cannot, we are convinced, cause an earlier one. Memory once again. Without memory, there can be no before and after, so either of the two events could be the cause and either could be the effect. Or, just conceivably, neither could be either.

LAST QUARTER

And time remembered is grief forgotten.

ALGERNON SWINBURNE

32

AFTER FOUR DAYS AND NIGHTS IN THE HOSPITAL, ON A BRIGHT, clear morning, Elizabeth was allowed to come home. When I called to collect her in the car they entrusted her to me only after I had signed for her like a parcel.

Dressed in the clothes that I had delivered the night before, she sat beside her bed on the visitors' chair, utterly motionless. I squatted down in front of her and looked into her eyes, clear and inanimate as glass marbles, bright, forgot-me blue. I took her pale, blank face gently between my hands and smiled with as much reassurance as I could simulate. Startlingly, her eyes came into focus and she smiled back.

'Hello,' she said. 'I love you, don't I?'

When the ward sister talked me through the elaborate schedule of medication, fully half of which seemed designed to counter the side-effects of the other half, she rattled each amber plastic bottle of pills before dropping it into a white paper bag, which she eventually handed to me with unconcealed professional reluctance, accompanied by stern warnings about the dangers of neglecting or exceeding any of the prescribed doses.

Elizabeth smiled all the way home beside me in the car, but it was an unchanging smile and she spoke not a word. I remembered how like a doll she had first appeared to me – a chilling memory to resurrect. As we neared the house she began peering intently through the windscreen, slumping down in her seat to gaze upwards into the horse chestnut trees shading the narrow lanes. Her expression was that of an infant in arms, examining the world for the first time, puzzled by the unfamiliarity of it all yet mysteriously convinced of its benevolence.

I led her by the hand from the car into our home – she betrayed no sign of having been there before – and I followed her from room to room while she gazed smilingly about her, pausing now and then to scrutinize some once-familiar object as though it were an unexpected gift. Each time this happened she would dart a sidelong glance at me and slip her arm through mine, seeming to seek my approval, or perhaps just making sure that I was still there. Whether or not she recognized me any more than she recognized her own possessions was impossible to tell, but she appeared some-how to sense that I *belonged* with her.

The weather that day was glorious, I remember, though cool for August, and when I sat her down in the garden among the overblown blooms she leaned back in the wicker-work chair, closed her eyes and drew in a long, rose-scented breath. I made tea for us both, and for the space of an afternoon everything became as it had been at the start, the two of us sitting in companionable silence amid the pastel blur of fallen petals, drowsing to the sound of industrious honey bees.

It continued like that for her, of course. Over the next four months, the pills – eighteen a day – kept her in a continuous state of torpid amiability. She slept for long periods during the day, like a cat, and the nights were peaceful and free of incident. She consumed without protest the meals I cooked for us both, but she ate without discrimination or obvious enjoyment, working her way methodically across the plate from one side to the other. Occasionally I would catch her looking at a forkful of food as though momentarily unsure of what she was meant to do with it, but I would gently steer it to her mouth where some automatic response would take over and she would eat on uncomplainingly until she had cleared her plate.

It might be imagined that this period of calm was a welcome respite for me, after the turbulence of life before, but in truth it began to depress me after a few weeks. Certainly Elizabeth was calm, but it was the tranquillity of the tranquillized, an unnatural, enforced placidity which I was disloyally imposing upon a mind which had always taken such delight in mental volatility, in jokes, mockery and spontaneous mischief. She smiled all the time, but she never once laughed.

There was one other problem. Now that she had given up her bouts of walking, her body was unable to burn up the energy in her food, so she began to put on weight. Within the space of four months she gained forty pounds. Her face

161

ballooned at the sides, leaving the features huddling together in the middle; her limbs puffed up so that her still-tiny feet looked like the tied-off ends on the legs of a rag doll.

There was a brief miracle which came about, appropriately enough, with the approach of Christmas. Elizabeth woke up one morning, looked hard at me, and clapped her hands.

'What are we doing, lying in bed?' she asked.

'What's wrong?' I replied warily.

'We must go out. We must go for a walk. A day like this we should be out walking.'

I looked out of the bedroom window at the frosted fields.

'All right,' I said, 'if you really feel up to it.'

I helped her to dress and we shared a pot of coffee before setting off up the lane. She gazed at everything, now turning her head slowly from side to side to take in the whole of that chilly landscape, now performing unsteady pirouettes of delight at being surrounded by it all. A spider's web, frost-etched against the darkness of the spinney, enraptured her for half an hour while she traced and retraced its spiralling complexity with one gloved fingertip.

Then it all went wrong. She started to move her hand faster and faster, her whole arm describing wild circles in the air until she herself began spinning as though caught up in a gathering whirlwind of her own making which, when it finally dashed her to the ground, squeezed from her lips a lingering shriek of anguish. She lay prone and spread-eagled on the frozen ground, staring wildly back over her shoulder towards her feet, her fingers scrabbling to gain a grip on the unyielding earth like a climber in mortal peril on a sheer vertical face. She had forgotten which way was up.

After I had walked her home – it took thirty-seven minutes of reasoned persuasion to overcome her mistrust of gravity – I lay her on our bed and she fell swiftly into a deep sleep. When I hung up her dressing-gown I found in the pockets dozens of her pills, clotted together in fluffy clumps, which she had obviously been spitting out and hiding over time whenever I wasn't looking. Not a miracle after all, then. I sat at the foot of the bed, listening to her slow, steady breathing, and I felt a surge, firstly of anger, then of loathing towards that sleeping, bloated form. The realization of that loathing startled and appalled me.

It was the loneliest moment of my life, not just because she was once more lost to me but because I was now rejecting her, conspiring in the loss. Having nobody who loved me was more bearable than having nobody to love. At that moment, love revealed itself to me as something that has really nothing to do with the feelings of any other person. I saw love as a thing which you can neither give nor receive, but only feel within yourself. You can never know for certain whether the loved one feels the same, and because you cannot know you can at least hope. But if there is no love within you for another, you know it and there can be no hope. No possible hope at all.

33

IT IS REMARKABLE HOW OFTEN WE USE THE WORD 'TIME' IN everyday conversation. We talk of 'having time' or of 'not having time' or of 'not having enough time' or of 'needing more time', much as we talk about money or food. We say 'it was a long time' or 'it was a short time' in the same way that we refer to a sentence or a rope. We can have a 'good time' or we can have a 'bad time', like we can have a good wine or a bad oyster. We can 'play for time' and we can 'make time' or 'find time'. We 'have no time' for those we despise, yet 'a lot of time' for those we admire and even 'all the time in the world' for those we love. We can 'mark time' and we can 'beat time' (a practice cautioned against by the Mad Hatter); we can 'waste time' and we can 'save time'. If we are lucky our bodies will not suffer the 'ravages of time', but if we are unlucky we may 'serve time' or even die 'before our time'. Events like birthdays happen to different people at 'different times', while the occurrence of a sunspot eruption happens to us all at the 'same time'. We speak of the 'pressure of time' as though referring to some gaseous or aqueous matter;

we find ourselves 'up against time' as though preparing for a fight. Time 'is the enemy', time 'will tell', time is 'the great physician' and 'the wisest of counsellors'. We treat points in time as though they were geographical locations so that we can be 'behind' time or 'on' time, 'between' times or just 'in' time. We talk of 'time lags', 'time warps' and 'time bombs' – just imagine the explosion of a bomb packed with time, spewing forth seconds and minutes in all directions. We take 'time out', work 'overtime', 'make up for lost time', 'gain time', 'buy time' (some advertising agencies actually employ people called 'time buyers') and it's 'high time' we recognized that we are talking about something which we do not, any more than did St Augustine, begin to understand. 'Time after time' and 'time and again' we refer to this thing called 'time' without giving it a second's thought, and doubtless we shall continue to do so until the last syllable of it has been recorded and all life has ceased.

I finished work on the watch in the small hours of a cold October morning and the moment of completion threw me into a quite unexpected spasm of physical distress. My eyes refused to focus and my hands shook violently for almost half an hour so that I was incapable even of winding the instrument to set it going. I have no idea what brought about this effect, although I imagine it was caused in part by my abrupt release from the pressure of concentration and also by a sudden fear of failure, by an acknowledgement, long suppressed, that behind that silver dial lay a mechanism in which the parts were so intricately interdependent that even the smallest of them, if flawed, could compromise the workings of the whole.

As my vision cleared, I seemed to see through the face of the watch into the works, as familiar to my fingers as the teeth in my mouth were to my tongue. I saw each screw, wheel and pinion, every jewel and arbor. I saw the springs and pallets and rollers, all still, waiting to be impelled into movement by the energy transferred from the muscles of my trembling hand through the winding crown to the mainspring. My eyes eventually focused on the tourbillon, static in anticipation of that impulse, and it struck me for the first time how uncanny it felt for a tourbillon, which in French can mean either 'whirlpool' or 'whirlwind', to be as motionless as a frozen waterfall.

I left the watch on the workshop bench and walked along a deserted Bond Street, through the Burlington Arcade and into Piccadilly, the cold air stinging my sinuses and squeezing tears from the corners of my eyes. A milk float rattled by on the other side of the road, its low electrical whine diminishing to nothing as it turned north into Dover Street. The traffic lights outside the Ritz changed in its wake. In the silence I was aware of the blood pulsing in my ears.

I have heard it said that all mammals enjoy roughly the same total number of heartbeats over the course of a lifetime. A mouse does not live very long but its heart beats far more quickly than that of a larger animal such as a dog. Elephants and humans, who live for many decades, have slower pulse

166

rates still. I have no idea whether the observation is true, but to me there is a satisfying tidiness to it, as though our internal organ of timing, our 'ticker', can somehow regulate the speed at which we live, determining the length of our natural lives. But what, ultimately, will give us in our final moments a sense of how long our lives have been? Not external measurements, not dates and records, but a reading of that subtler, if less reliable instrument — memory.

Recent research at Duke University in North Carolina suggests that we may have an inbuilt mental timepiece, hard-wired into the cerebral cortex. Spiny neurons in the forebrain are triggered by shots of dopamine fired by bunches of cortical neurons at the start of any activity, and this seems to set in motion an internal pendulum of sorts. People involved in serious accidents may experience a rush of dopamine which speeds up the timing mechanism, giving them the illusion that the world around them has gone into slow motion. Similarly, as we grow older and our dopamine levels drop, the pendulum may slow and time appear to run more quickly. When I first read about this I was inevitably reminded of that conversation with Elizabeth all those years ago about ageing and our different perceptions of the speed of passing time, and I ached for just a moment to return to that restaurant table and share the new theory with her.

I returned to the workshop and wound the watch. The tourbillon began to rotate and the second hand set off on its first sweep across the Roman numerals. When I held the case to my ear the tick sounded clean and true. It worked. It did the job. It told the time. Or rather, it told *a* time. Which time it told I had yet to determine, but at least I knew that, within the confines of its own mechanical universe, it told its own time.

34

ELIZABETH'S CONDITION DETERIORATED SO MUCH IN THE WEEKS
following her collapse in the lane that in January I was
compelled through sheer exhaustion to find a residential
nursing home for her. She could no longer recognize me
or her surroundings. She did not comprehend the purpose of
our furniture, could not dress herself, not being able to
identify her clothes. She showed no sign of understanding,
nor even of really hearing, anything I said to her. Her speech
had deserted her entirely, to the point where she no longer
made any attempt to communicate. She now had great
difficulty in walking, having seemingly forgotten how her
legs worked, and there was a terrifying emptiness in her eyes,
a bleary unblinking gaze that seemed forever focused on
some impossibly distant and worrying horizon.

She was obliviously incontinent, drooling in a fireside
chair, her bladder emptying itself at unpredictable intervals,
the fluid pooling on the boards beneath. It was hard to feed
her because, although she would allow me without protest to
coax a spoonful of food between her lips, she had forgotten
how to chew, and the food would remain in her mouth until

she began to choke and I would have to prise open her jaws and scoop out the soggy mess with my fingers. She began to smell bad; a sour odour of decay and putrefaction which no amount of my bathing her would overcome. It was like having to tend an exhumed cadaver.

They brought a wheelchair for Elizabeth and shut us both in the back of a private ambulance, which reeked oddly of stale cigarette smoke. The home, on the outskirts of the nearby county town, had been recommended without enthusiasm by our local doctor. It was a large Edwardian house, a preposterous three-storey concoction of red brick, festooned with white wooden balconies, cream stone quoins and oriel windows. In the entrance hall, with its black-and-white tiled floor, there was an overpowering smell of disinfectant and boiled mince and a constant babble of muffled cries and howls from somewhere up above.

An aged, hesitant lift carried us up to the first floor, where two nurses undressed her, draped her in a plain cotton shift and laid her on a narrow bed in a pale green room devoid of decoration save for a faded reproduction of a row of poplar trees. There was a free-standing wash basin in the corner of the room, and the uncurtained window looked out onto a dense clump of dark laurels. None of which really mattered to Elizabeth, whose conscious mind was well beyond the reach of her surroundings, however impoverished or grim. But it depressed me beyond measure. I sat with her for an hour, holding her hand, but her eyes, wet and red-rimmed because her blinking reflex had begun to fail, remained empty and unfocused. When I left she had curled herself into a foetal position and was rocking slowly back and forth.

At first I visited her every day, but there was no apparent benefit to her from my presence. The staff were solicitous but tired. The most they could say was that Elizabeth was no worse, but then how could they know? How could any of us know what might or might not have been happening inside that locked and crippled mind? She seemed unchanged and unchanging, but we all knew that the deterioration had not ceased, that it would continue now through all eternity. There was no more chance of her brain repairing itself than of the broken wine glass spontaneously reassembling. Things fall apart, not together.

My visits became fewer, sometimes as much as a week passing between them, so each time I saw her there were fresh signs of degeneration. She became distressingly thin, her feet poking out from beneath the shift were like those of some desiccated reptile. She could move only her head, a purpose-less, rotating motion which she could keep up for hours on end, and which had worn all the hair from the back of her scalp. To prevent pressure sores she had to be constantly moved and anointed with barrier cream. Even the stinging, penetrating odour of disinfectant could not conceal the fetor of terminal corruption escaping from her ruined flesh.

My emotional dissociation from her was complete and so, therefore, was my guilt. I could not pity her, I could not find anything in or about her upon which to fasten my sympathy. All that I could pity was the person she once had been, the

171

person I remembered having loved more than anything in the world. But if there could not be pity, there most certainly could be horror, a horror born of wondering whether from the beginning she had perhaps been conscious of everything that was happening to her. I remembered what Gonzalez, the neuropsychologist, had told me, that when the final stages came I would never know whether she was, as she now seemed, unaware of the catastrophe which had overtaken her or whether her damaged brain still possessed awareness, but had cruelly stripped her of the physical means of communicating any response, leaving her like a lunatic being slowly torn to pieces in a soundproof room.

Following a four-day gap between visits, I walked into her room one morning and found a stranger with her, a frail, twitching old man in brown flannel pyjamas, crouching at the foot of the bed, one bony hand thrust up inside her bed gown while the other scrabbled away at his own crotch. He turned and paused when he heard me enter the room and gave me a vacant smile before resuming his fervid rummaging. I grasped his arms and pulled him away, out into the corridor. He did not resist. He just grinned and winked at me and let out a wheezy gust of conspiratorial laughter. The nurses scolded him and he cowered, wrapping both arms over the top of his head like a confused gibbon. They led him away to wherever he was supposed to be.

I returned to Elizabeth, overwhelmed by a sense of bleak futility and filled with loathing for all humankind. How could that form which lay on the bed, that form which had once been the most adorable of beings, possibly stimulate the lust of any creature? As I moved to cover her up, I saw dark blood on the sheet and, peeling back her gown, I found a suppurating bedsore on her hip the size of a teacup. It was a deep, beetroot red with ragged yellow edges, and at its centre, blue-tinged and shiny, the bone unmistakably protruded. I had her transferred to a private hospital before the morning's end.

35

TESTING THE ACCURACY OF ANY TIMEPIECE IS A PROBLEMATIC business, even setting aside the fundamental consideration as to what it is to be tested *against*. During the nineteenth century, testing laboratories and observatories were operating in, among other places, Hamburg, Washington, Geneva, Neuchâtel and Kew – the last being succeeded by the National Physical Laboratory at Teddington, home of the airborne atomic clock. Since there was almost no uniformity of approach or interpretation between the different testing centres, and since each laboratory was continuously striving to improve its own measurements, it was impossible to establish any common standard. The foundation for a universally accepted system was eventually laid in 1873 at the first of the Geneva Observatory's annual chronometer competitions, but the early rules were constantly being amended, right up to their final 1957 form, to accommodate technical advances made over the years.

In terms of hard numbers, the accuracy of a watch is defined in two ways: first according to its rate and second its fluctuations. If the watch under trial 'loses' five seconds a day, but it loses that amount consistently, then it is regarded as accurate. Its readings do not have to be in agreement with those of the test instrument: they merely need to differ by a precise and predictable amount. It is the fluctuations of rate which represent 'inaccuracy' in a watch, and those fluctuations may be caused by factors such as position, temperature and gravity.

In competition, a category 'A' Deck Watch of the kind I had constructed would normally be tested over a period of forty-four days, much longer than the normal testing period required for the assignment of the 'Geneva Seal' which confers chronometer status on an instrument. To establish its rate, the watch may be tested in six different positions, dial-up and dial-down, as well as pendant-up, -left, -right and -down. Its mean daily rate will be assessed, as will its mean daily variation rate, from position to position. The difference will be measured between its mean rate when dial-up and pendant-up, and the variation of rate will be noted for each Celsius degree of temperature change. It will be seen from this that there is a high degree of rigour in the competition's testing methods, and it was without expectation of immediate success that I began running the initial workshop tests. At this stage I was comfortably resigned to dismantling and rebuilding the watch many times before it would achieve anything like true timekeeping.

The acoustic timing machine that we use in the workshop is an old and trusted servant which provides a quick, preliminary test of a watch's accuracy. It is in essence a listening device, which 'hears' the tick of the watch and compares it to an electronically generated quartz pulse of its own. The reading is printed out on a long, narrow roll of paper, like a supermarket till roll, and takes the form of a trail of dots representing the 'ticks' of the watch. With a perfectly accurate instrument (or, rather, one which agrees with the machine's own notion of the time) the dotted trace will run dead straight, parallel to the edge of the paper. Any deviation in rate will cause the trace to stray gently towards one margin or the other, depending on whether the watch is running fast or slow. The machine has such a sensitive ear that it cannot be used to check pendulum clocks, or any clock with a frictional rest escapement, because there is just too much extraneous noise thrown off by the mechanism and this creates a scrambled printout.

I attached the acoustic pickup to the watch, clamped the assembly to the bench and switched on the machine. Greatly to my astonishment, the trace, after an initial, unsettling bout of apparently random oscillation, ran straight down the centre of the paper, not a dot venturing out of line to left or right. This happened in each of the first five positions. In all five tests, which I ran for three minutes apiece, the trace was an identical arrow-straight line. I can hardly convey to anyone unversed in watch lore what a very unlikely result this was, so unlikely in fact that there was a distinct odour of the miraculous about it, or of the occult.

In the sixth position, dial-down, the trace drifted percept-ibly away to one side, indicating that, in this position, the watch was running slow. This result put me into something of a quandary. Gazely's great standard work on watchmaking lists no fewer than 115 possible causes of bad timekeeping in a watch, including seventeen potential problems with the balance assembly alone. Were I to dismantle the watch in order to discover the cause of the error, might I not also disturb one or more of the other flawless conjunctions which demonstrably existed within the mechanism? The fault would have been more perplexing had it occurred in one of the pendant positions, since the tourbillon should equal out all such errors, but in either the dial-up or dial-down position there was a clear possibility that some microscopic inequality of friction between the two balance-staff pivots and the jewelled bearings in which they sat was causing the retardation of the mechanism.

Warily, I opened the back of the case and studied the intricacies of the mechanism within. As I took up my eyeglass and contemplated the regular blurring of the hairspring beneath the swinging balance wheel and the slow revolution of the surrounding tourbillon, some flicker of superstition made me close the watch again without making any alteration. I attached it once more, dial-down, to the bench, switched on the timing machine and now the watch ran true. Many a watchmaker can relate similar experiences, where the simple act of looking critically at a faulty movement seems capable of correcting the error, as though some physical interference were brought to bear upon the mechanism through the mere act of examination.

The timing machine, however, provides a reading only of how an instrument performs at a particular point in time. The watch now had to be put through the full battery of tests over a forty-four-day period. We shared the vigil between the three of us – myself and the two partners, who, having replicated for themselves my initial test results, regarded and handled the instrument with a degree of reverence which would scarcely have been excessive in pilgrims confronted with an authenticated fragment of the True Cross.

During those days I found myself increasingly at a loose end. After five years and seven months of continuous work on the watch, its completion had removed the core of my life, and I found myself wishing, perversely, that the instrument would reveal some imperfection which would require me to resume my labours. But it was not to be. At the end of almost a month and a half of ceaseless interrogation, the watch ran as true as ever. Testing in an oven at 33°C produced errors, of course, as did refrigeration down to 4°C, but these we were able to cope with by judicious manipulation of the appropriate compensation screws on the balance rim (there was no detectable middle-temperature error). At the end of our trials, in the course of which the Breguet-pattern sweep hand had ticked off more than 3.8 million seconds, it still appeared to hit its mark in synchronization both with the BBC broadcast time signal and the cheap radio-controlled wall clock which we had bought from a mail-order catalogue just for testing purposes. (Our age must surely be the first in which cheap goods outperform expensive ones, when a factory-produced

£20 novelty clock may outperform, in terms of accuracy, a hand-built mechanical movement which may have taken a master craftsman five years to build.)

When I note that the watch 'appeared' to display a synchronous reading with those other instruments, I am indicating a problem which becomes apparent only with the demand for extreme degrees of accuracy. The problem is one of – we come to it once more – perception. If I attempted to determine whether the watch was accurate to, let us say, one second in a thousand years – not an unreasonable enterprise – could I detect deviation on so small a scale with just the human eye?

The space on the watch face between each of the minute indicators was one-sixtieth of the circumference, something like 4mm, and the tip of the hand covered that distance, or so it appeared, in one second. Assuming the watch were to lose one second over the next thousand years (encompassing 243 leap years), this would represent a loss of one unit in roughly 31.5 billion. Averaged out, the time lost by the watch over the course of each minute would equate, roughly, to 0.0000027 of a second, far less than the blink of an eye, resulting in the second hand when it reached the twelve o'clock position being in retard against the dial by one hundred-thousandth of a millimetre, a distance shorter than the wavelength of any visible light. In these microscopic regions the human eye is an untrustworthy guide.

I took the watch to Geneva, cradling it in my lap during the flight, and submitted it for testing at the Institut Horologique, where they have access not only to electron microscopes and laser scanners but also to the full resources of the community of commercial watchbuilders. During the six days of testing I took the opportunity to visit a number of factories, catching up with old contacts, but there was little of interest going on save at Patek Philippe where, in one of their *ateliers des pièces spéciales*, they were overhauling one of their instruments of *grande complication*. Not only was it built to perform the expected additional functions of showing sidereal time (with separate equation dial) and the phases of the moon but the leap-year mechanism had been constructed to recognize the 'omitted' leap years as established in 1582 by Pope Gregory XIII, who laid down that only such centennial years as were exactly divisible by 400 should benefit from the extra day.

When I returned to the Institut I was hailed as a phenomenon. The aloof, slightly mocking technicians who had taken the watch from me six days previously were now gratifyingly deferential, falling over each other in their anxiety to show me their different test results. All had reached the same conclusion. Within the sensitivities of the test equipment available to them, including the atomic clocks, the watch kept perfect time. The director, a plump and surprisingly boisterous man with a magnificent moustache, insisted on my staying one more night in Geneva (entirely at the Institut's expense), and took a party of us by taxi to a splendid restaurant near Lausanne where we drank far too many toasts to one another in a Swiss white wine which I am almost sure was called Chemin de Fer.

Over coffee the subject of pulsars was raised and the director adopted a grave expression, saying, '*Alors, oui c'est vrai*, there we have a problem. We know the rate of our caesium clocks against the pulsars and, *franchement*, your watch is not good . . .' He stared down into his cup for a second, sensing my discomfort in the sudden silence, then looked up with a smile of pure mischief on his lips and went on, 'Nor is it bad.' He laughed and punched me gently on the shoulder. 'Let me quickly explain what I mean.'

'I would be grateful,' I told him.

'So, pulsars, yes? There are perhaps fifty of them that we know about and they are maybe the most precise timekeepers in the universe. But they do not all agree with each other, so we have been working with the people in Paris and at Teddington, and with the US Navy's hydrogen maser clock in Washington, to get some kind of consensus, some calibration between two or three pulsars.'

'I knew that some such work was going on,' I told him, 'but I had no idea what progress had been made.'

'We are very close to establishing a Pulsar Mean Time, as you might call it,' he replied, 'and your watch runs close to that mean, but not precisely on it. In other words, it does not agree with any one of the pulsars. Sloppy workmanship, I would call it . . .' And he collapsed in a gale of cognac-fuelled mirth.

I flew back to London the following morning with a pitiless hangover and the uneasy, nagging feeling that I had, in building the watch, done something very wrong.

36

THEY HAD TAKEN THE FEEDING TUBE OUT OF HER NOSE BECAUSE
she kept thrashing her head from side to side, tearing the
lining of her nasal cavity. (Who were they? I no longer saw
them as individuals, but as a homogeneous white mass of
medical indifference.) The tube was now connected directly
to her stomach through a hole in her side. The food, a pale
yellow fluid with the frothy viscosity of beaten egg, was
poured into the raised end of the tube through a funnel
and bubbled its way down into her body. They encouraged
me to feed her, but on the two or three occasions I attempted
it the task proved more exacting than I had anticipated. The
level of liquid had to be carefully controlled because too swift
a flow would cause the food to back up inside her oesophagus
– the trick of peristalsis had been lost – threatening to choke
her. They had treated and dressed the pressure sores (the
others had been on her right heel and at the base of her
spine), but there was a serious risk, they told me, of septi-
caemia, not just from the sores but from other infections
introduced through the feeding tube or bladder catheter. She
had lost almost all of her hair from rubbing her head on the

pillow, and beneath the yellow skin of her body all the fat had melted away, even the tiny pad on the bridge of her nose – this last gave her face a pinched, beaky aspect like that of a reproachful raptor.

Whereas before, in the nursing home, I had been prepared to believe that there was some consciousness within her of what was happening, now I was convinced that she was mercifully free of any such awareness. It was as though in the course of that long decline her mind had been deliberately and methodically loosed from all its moorings in the world, left to drift in a timeless void, unable to give things the necessary shape which makes sense of them. With the disintegration of memory had come the loss not just of personality but of all intuition of time, space and causality, and, without these inbuilt filters to winnow the data harvested by our senses, we can make nothing of the world.

Her eyes were no longer the bright windows of her being, not from either side. Those watery pale blue discs offered no expression of internal animation, and seemed incapable of admitting even the merest flicker of light from the outside for onward transmission to whatever vestigial mental processes persisted within. Elizabeth no longer dwelt in time or space; there was nothing inside and so there was nothing outside.

Sitting with her one morning, listening as always to her breathing – some frail circuit still managing to trigger the reflex – I was jarred by the curious and disorienting sensation that it was I, not she, who had gone away. I was no longer there, neither I nor my universe. I now believe I experienced some

183

kind of fit, some cerebral equivalent of hysterical blindness. Everything around me, the insipid hospital room with its pale pine furniture, its Nile-green plastic curtains, its scuffed linoleum and its jumble of tubes and cables, and everything outside, beyond the windows, every squirrel and growing blade of grass, the very sky itself – I knew with literally blinding certainty that they were no longer there. And I felt a huge rush of knowing, just for an instant, what it would truly be like *not to be*. It was a feeling of such terrifying exhilaration that I rose involuntarily out of the chair with my arms outstretched and my mouth gaping open at the blankness all around me. In my mind's eye there was nothing of me and nothing of anything else. It was not the unbearable roar on the other side of silence; it was the *silence* on the other side of silence.

That was the night she died, the night I forgot my watch. They told me that the final cause of death was an unidentified infection. Her temperature had risen rapidly during the course of the afternoon and it was all over in a matter of hours. I asked to see the body and they told me that they were proposing a post-mortem examination to confirm the dementia. They led me down to the basement mortuary where her body had been laid out under a sheet on a stainless-steel table, and uncovered it for me.

It was an affecting moment, though in a quite unexpected way. I am not sure what I had been anticipating – shock, perhaps, or revulsion, but I felt neither. Looking down at that sear and uninhabited husk, I felt at last a surging wave of the pity which I had been unable for so long to summon forth.

Pity not for myself, nor for the wreckage which lay before me, but, once more, pity for the person she had been. Pity and anguish and a soaring joy in our joint liberation from the unremitting years of torment. I gave them permission for the autopsy. Anything of her they could damage was long gone.

The funeral was, predictably, something of a charade, although a tolerable enough one. The rector recited the usual reassurances about the inevitability of suffering in this life and the absence of it in the life hereafter. He had carefully composed a short word-picture of Elizabeth's personality before the onset of the illness, how charming and full of life she had been, and I was moved by his diligence and grateful for his compassion. Had Elizabeth been there to hear it, she and I might have exchanged cynical glances – he had, after all, hardly known her – but in her absence I could not make the effort to be cynical. A handful of people from the village had turned up and, nineteen minutes into the service, Charlotte slid into the front pew beside me, stepping heavily on my foot and wreathing me in some pugnaciously musky scent.

When the service ended, everybody shuffled round to the village pub and I bought us all drinks and thick, comforting sandwiches. The villagers drifted away in twos and threes, and, when we were alone, Charlotte asked, 'Was it pretty fucking shitty? I mean, at the end?'

'It was . . . yes, that just about covers it.'

'You poor old poppet. Sorry I never came to see her. I'm bloody useless at hospitals and stuff.'

'It's all right. For the last few months she wouldn't have

known you.' I took a sip of beer and asked, 'How's the old wound?'

She winced and hunched up on one side. 'I got some-thing called a frozen shoulder. Sounds like a piece of New Zealand lamb, doesn't it? But it's a real bugger, take it from me.'

'Can they fix it?'

'Seems not. I shall probably take it to my grave. Whoops, sorry about that.'

And in spite of everything, or maybe just because of everything, I laughed.

'How's your electrician?' I asked her.

'Who?' She looked puzzled. 'Oh, him. No, that was all over centuries ago. I'm strictly celibate right now. Not entirely from choice, I might add. A good man may be hard to find, but the other sort is fucking impossible. Don't fancy having a stab at it, do you?'

'Charlotte, I'm shocked,' I said, and I was.

She shrugged and instantly regretted it, wincing again at her shoulder.

'A fuck's a fuck, poppet. Only trying to cheer you up.'

'I'm very touched, Charlotte, but I think I need some time to come to terms with everything. I've been living such a weird life for so long that I'm afraid you're a bit much for me right now.'

'Lizzie was my very best friend. I owe it to her to look after you. Make sure you don't mope. After all, you saved her life and we were all grateful as hell.'

'I'm sorry,' I responded, mystified. 'In what sense can I be said to have saved her life?'

'Literally. Before she met you, we were all convinced she was going to top herself. She'd made a couple of attempts at it.'

'I had no idea. What happened?'

'Oh, silly stuff with razor blades, pills, that sort of thing. She swam out to sea once at West Wittering and they had to send a helicopter up to find her.'

'But she was always laughing, always. She never seemed to be taking anything that seriously.'

'All your doing, poppet. You were just what she needed after that bastard dumped her.'

'What was he like?'

'He was, as dear old Malcolm might have put it, an egregious wanker of the first water. We all begged her not to marry him, we could all see how it would end up, but she did it anyway.'

'What was wrong with him?'

'Thick.'

'He was stupid? But I thought he was some sort of electronics genius.'

'He was a computer salesman. Thick as pigshit. That's why he buggered off in the end. She was just too bright for him and it made him feel small. He was forever coming out with these really naff opinions and she'd send him up something rotten. He was too dim to realize what she was up to at first, but it got through to him in the end and he couldn't bear it. I think he finally shacked up with a traffic warden or maybe she was a dancer.'

'But she was always taking the piss out of me, too. There was no malice in it, it was just fun.'

'Ah, but you've got a brain, poppet, and you know you're one of nature's brightest and best. He was just a dumb blond and she never let him forget it.'

'She once told me that he left her because she was too nice.'

'Likely sounding tale, or what? No, he ran away because he couldn't keep up with her intellectually. Not, mind you, that any of us ever could. She had the finest brain I've ever come across, present company included.' She knocked back her drink and scooped up her handbag. 'Keep in touch. Time is all it takes.'

'Time is all what takes?' I asked, bemused.

'Everything,' she said with a throaty chuckle. And she was gone.

Reality, normal life. That was what was happening to me. I felt, I supposed, how men must feel returning from war, unready to exchange a world of drab fearful horrors for one of tentatively optimistic normality. I felt like someone feels who spends a bright summer's afternoon in a dark, smoky cinema, engrossed in some tenebrous gothic drama, only to emerge blinking into a world where it is still broad daylight and where there are shops and children and safety and laughter and people getting on with their lives.

Do I trivialize my recovery into that new, real world? I do not think so. Grief is what usually, and constantly, hampers the progression back to normality, but grief was not something that afflicted me. For me the grieving had been endured before the bereaving, doled out to me minute by minute, day by day, year by year – mustardspoonsful of gall. Now I could grieve no more. All I could do was keep the memory alive and love that memory.

37

WEEKS AFTER MY RETURN FROM GENEVA, THE WATCH CONTINUED
to produce in me an unwelcome sense of superstitious
unease, of dread almost. Word had spread from Switzerland
and I was assailed daily from all parts of the world by
congratulatory messages and invitations to show the watch
and talk about it at horological conferences and seminars.
Museums and observatories clamoured for sight of the
miraculous instrument, watchmakers begged for a glimpse
of its movement. Yet for all its perfection, I knew that the
watch was somehow wrong, not in itself, but in what it was
doing. I carried it with me everywhere, partly from fear of
having it stolen – not by some ignorant chancer but by
another watchmaker whose obsession to *know* had become
too much to bear. I carried it in a padded shoulder pouch,
slung across my body, careful to protect it from any sudden
jolt that might cause the escapement to set. I checked it
infrequently now, but when I did, it still ran as true as I was
able to measure. It hung heavily on me and filled my dreams.

The revelation came to me as I squatted on the grass at the
foot of Elizabeth's grave. I must confess that I had neglected

the spot shamefully and it had been heavy work hacking away the nettles and brambles which had grown up over her. So as not to disturb the watch while I worked, I had taken it from its pouch and propped it against the headstone. Now, as I stood looking down at it, the true underlying source of my disquietude began to formulate itself in my mind.

I have mentioned that the graveyard straddles the Meridian line, and so, in common with the observatory at Greenwich, marks the place where it is decreed that the first instant of each new day begins on the planet, and for as long as the convention persists this will always be so, however much the earth may slow in its rotation. Even were a new Meridian line to be internationally agreed, the old one, like every other longitudinal line, would continue moving round in step, as the earth persisted in telling its own correct solar time. The Horizontal Instrument would still be the most durably accurate timekeeper on earth, and what was Elizabeth's grave but another Horizontal Instrument?

What had been nagging at my conscience was that the watch, the watch begun because I could never know the exact time of her death, the miraculous watch that owed its very existence to her memory, was betraying that memory with its precision, was being false to that memory by telling a time which was not *her* time, a time which would never be her time, a time which would diverge ever further from the true time marked by her resting place, making a mockery of that stone which spoke glibly of loving memory.

All through that night I contemplated the problem of

191

divergence from many angles, not wholly unaware that there was something a little irrational in my frenzy for this reconciliation. My initial thought was simply to allow the watch to run down, never to be rewound, so putting an end once and for all to its presumption of accuracy; I also considered, if only fleetingly, destroying the watch altogether. Either course would make the reconciliation problem cease to exist, but neither would solve it, and I was intent on a solution, not a capitulation.

Inevitably, my thoughts turned to the possibility of introducing an index into the movement as a means of retarding the mechanism. An index is the small movable pointer to be found above the balance cock; to one side of it are engraved the letters F and/or A, standing for 'fast' or '*avance*', and to the other the letters S and/or R for 'slow' or '*retard*'. The two pins which protrude from the underside of the index pass through the balance cock to grasp the overcoil of the balance spring (with an overcoil there is arguably no necessity for a turn-boot), and so, by moving the pointer to one side or the other, the rate of the watch can be regulated. When Max Studer established the precision timing record in 1962, with that Patek Philippe movement No. 198 411, by dispensing with index regulation in favour of a free-sprung balance spring, he was aspiring to heights of accuracy from which I was attempting to descend. An index would represent a small spanner in my works. The question was, could it possibly be small enough?

If my plan were to match the watch's rate to the earth's

solar time, not just for one month or one year but for centuries to come, what amount of retardation would be necessary? Remembering that in the last forty years the Paris atomic clock has 'gained' thirty seconds on all Horizontal Instruments, I calculated that I should have to cause the watch to run slow at an average rate of around three-quarters of a second per year, or 0.0020548 seconds per day – although, by taking the average, I was tacitly accepting a constant rate of deceleration. If the planet were not just slowing but slowing more with each successive rotation, like a roulette wheel, or slowing by an increasing or decreasing amount each year, the mechanical means of replicating such behaviour could prove so complicated as to be beyond my capabilities as a watchmaker. And were the planet to begin speeding up again, the problem would be, I was convinced, insoluble.

Even to contemplate such a refinement would mean collaborating with the Institut in Geneva, since I would need not only their ingenuity in design but also their finer calculations in determining the degree of deviation from Pulsar Mean Time. I was nervous of their reaction to my plan, which they might well see as an act of vandalism; and, sure enough, as I outlined it over the telephone to the director, I was conscious of a growing silence at the other end of the line. I waited for his reaction, listening to the sound of his breath whistling through his moustache.

Eventually he said, 'This can be done, I think. But you know, to me, as a good Swiss, you are speaking heresy – blasphemy, maybe. To want to make a watch less accurate, *c'est inouï* . . . but it can be done, and I shall show you how. All I ask is that you tell me why you want to do this thing. I am in London in two weeks, we should meet and drink some warm beer.'

And sixteen days later I met him off the train and drove him back to the village.

We sat together on the flint wall of the churchyard while I told him about Elizabeth and the Horizontal Instrument, and he smiled gently, nodded and patted my arm.

'Tell me,' he asked, 'for how long does this fine watch of yours need to show this horizontal time?'

'Not for ever,' I said. 'Just while I am alive.'

'And after?'

I looked round into his earnest, twinkling eyes.

'After, the Institut shall have it,' I told him.

With a sigh, he picked up the slim black leather briefcase which had been leaning against the wall and passed me a sheaf of mechanical drawings.

'This will work,' he said. 'But only up to a point. You will have to accept that we are working here with averages. If the earth carries on the way it has been going over the past forty years then, over time, this will work.'

As I glanced through the drawings, he rose to his feet, sniffed the air and, rubbing his hands together, said, 'So where is this pub?'

I pointed it out to him and he said, 'I shall see you there later. I think maybe you would like to be here on your own for a little while. I will order you a nice warm beer.'

There was an odd little smile on his face, and I must somehow have betrayed my curiosity because he added, 'I also have lost my wife, and I am always remembering her.'

I nodded and he asked me, 'Do you believe in God at all?'

'Not really, I'm afraid.'

'There has been an interesting theological debate going on for some centuries now as to whether or not God exists *in* time, or whether, being eternal and omnipresent, He exists somehow *beyond* time. Does anything strike you as peculiar about this idea of a deity for whom time means nothing?'

'It can only mean', I answered after some consideration, 'that such a God would have no memory.'

'Now there's a comforting thought for us poor sinners,' he said and strolled off, calling back over his shoulder, 'Take your time. Take all the time you want.'

I sat by the grave and looked at the drawings in detail. It was an ingenious solution they had come up with, even by the standards of men who as long ago as 1927 had developed that mechanism for skipping over the 29th of February in the year 2100. Technically, what they proposed was the introduction of a series of interacting wheels which every four years would bring about, at precisely noon on Christmas day (an elegant touch), a three-second pause in the running of the movement; a Swiss railway clock hiatus, only longer, which would keep the watch in synchronization with Coordinated Universal Time. I noted with some amusement that the design would allow them to remove the mechanism after my death and restore the watch to its original state of perfection. I began work on it the following day.

It will not be perfect, nor could it be, nor for that matter do I want it to be, but it will be a watch on a quest, just as I had imagined all those years ago – a watch that will be forever 'hunting' either side of its mark. It will rarely be in exact agreement with the solar time marked by Elizabeth's earth but, so long as the two of them swing back and forth, as in a dance, sometimes fast, sometimes slow, the pair will now and then touch hands before rebounding away again into the dark. And every four years, as it draws too far away, the watch will check itself and retrace its steps back to its partner on the dance floor.

It was memory which had brought all this to pass, memory which has told this story. It is memory which now brings back those bright, forget-me-not blue eyes to gaze into my own inner eye, and memory which brandishes the image of dried blood in a nostril torn by a ripped-out feeding tube. Memory is the thing that tells us who we are; memory is all we know. Music is memory, love is memory. There is no present moment; there is only the freshest memory. As I said at the outset, time is memory. But then so is everything else.

ACKNOWLEDGEMENTS

FOR THE STORY OF THE HORIZONTAL INSTRUMENT, AND INDEED THE knowledge of its very existence, I am indebted to A. J. Turner's collection of scholarly papers, *Of Time and Measurement* (Variorum), as I am for much other information about dialling and early timekeeping. Details of the traditional watchmaking process were plundered mostly from the late W. J. Gazely's *Watch and Clock Making and Repairing* (Robert Hale), with occasional resort to F. W. Britten's *Horological Hints and Helps* (Antique Collectors' Club). For information on the history and construction of Swiss watches, I relied heavily on *Patek Philippe* by Martin Huber and Alan Banbery (Verlag Peter Ineichen), on *Breguet, Watchmakers Since 1775* by Emmanuel Breguet (Alain de Gourcuff) and to a lesser extent on *Chronograph, Wristwatches to Stop Time* by Gerd-R. Lang and Reinhard Meis (Schiffer). On the philosophy of time, I leaned on Huw Price's *Time's Arrow and Archimedes' Point* (Oxford) and on Henri Bergson's *Matter and Memory* (translated by N. M. Paul and W. S. Palmer, Zone Books) from which the novel's opening quotation is taken. The St Augustine references are in the form quoted by Bertrand Russell in his *History of Western Philosophy* (Routledge). My awareness of the problems associated with dementia came initially from the chapter on Alzheimer's disease in Sherwin B. Nuland's *How We Die* (Chatto & Windus) and later from *The 36-Hour Day* (Hodder & Stoughton with Age Concern), which seems to me an invaluable book for anyone coping at home with a dementia sufferer. The stuff about atomic clocks and binary pulsars came from John Gribbin's *Companion to the Cosmos* (Weidenfeld & Nicolson). The Institut Horologique in Geneva is a fabrication, and if there is a real one, no resemblance to the staff should be inferred. Finally, I am grateful to Dr Joan Furlong of the National Physical Laboratory, Teddington, for her patience in correcting a number of my own early misconceptions about planetary rotation and time measurement and for providing me with up-to-date information about the state of contemporary horology. If any of the science in the novel is wrong, this may be put down to artistic licence or, more probably, ignorance.

CW